Poor work

This bo
ely

Poor work

DISADVANTAGE AND THE
DIVISION OF LABOUR

Edited by
PHILLIP BROWN AND RICHARD SCASE

Open University Press
Milton Keynes · Philadelphia

Open University Press
Celtic Court
22 Ballmoor
Buckingham
MK18 1XW

and
1900 Frost Road, Suite 101
Bristol, PA 19007, USA

First published 1991

British Library Cataloguing in Publication Data

Poor work: disadvantage and the division of labour.
 1. Division of labour. Sociological perspectives
 I. Brown, Phillip 1957–   II. Scase, Richard
 306.36

 ISBN 0–335–09941–6
 ISBN 0–335–09940–8 (pbk)

Library of Congress Cataloging-in-Publication Data

Poor work:disadvantage and the division of labour/edited by
 Phillip Brown and Richard Scase.
   p.   cm.
 Includes index.
  ISBN 0–335–09941–6 – ISBN 0–335–09940–8 (pbk)
  1. Underemployment. 2. Handicapped – Employment. 3. Minorities –
Employment. 4. Women – Employment. 5. Youth – Employment.
I. Brown, Phillip, 1957–   . II. Scase, Richard.
HD5709.P66   1991
331.1 – dc20
                                                    90-45381
                                                       CIP

Typeset by Scarborough Typesetting Services
Printed in Great Britain by St Edmundsbury Press Limited
Bury St Edmunds, Suffolk

Contents

Notes on contributors

David N. Ashton is Professor of Sociology and Director of Research of the Labour Market Studies Group, University of Leicester. In 1989–90 he was Visiting Professor, Department of Sociology, University of Alberta. He has published widely in the field of labour markets and the school–to–work transition. His latest books are *Restructuring the Labour Market: The Implications for Youth* (with M. J. Maguire and M. Spilsbury) (Macmillan) and *Making Their Way, Education, Training and the Labour Market in Canada and Britain* (co-edited with G. S. Lowe) (Open University Press).

Phillip Brown is a Lecturer in Sociology at the University of Kent at Canterbury. His publications include *Schooling Ordinary Kids* and he has edited a number of volumes including *Beyond Thatcherism: Social Policy, Politics and Society* (with R. Sparks) (Open University Press). He is currently writing a book on education, economy and society.

Malcolm Cross is currently Principal Research Fellow at the Centre for Research in Ethnic Relations at the University of Warwick. He has written or edited more than a dozen books and more than a hundred chapters, articles or reports. He has been chairperson of both the British Sociological Association and the Social Research Association and is currently editor of *New Community: a journal of research and policy on ethnic relations*.

Hartley Dean is a Research Fellow in Social Policy at the University of Kent and is currently engaged on an ESRC-funded project – 'Dependency Culture: the Image and Reality of the Claiming Process'. Having previously spent twelve years as an advice centre worker in Brixton, his particular interests are social security, housing and tribunals. He is author of *Social Security and Social Control* (Routledge).

Ralph Fevre is a Lecturer in Sociology at University College of Swansea. He has previously worked at Portsmouth Polytechnic. His publications include

Cheap Labour and Racial Discrimination (Gower) and *Wales is Closed* (Spokesman). He is currently working on a new textbook on *The Sociology of Labour Markets*.

C. C. Harris is Professor of Sociology at University College, Swansea. He has published widely on the family, notably *The Family and Industrial Society* (Unwin Hyman). His most recent publications are *Redundancy and Recession* (Blackwell) and *Kinship* (Open University Press).

David Lee studied at the London School of Economics and Birmingham University, and is now Senior Lecturer at the University of Essex. He has written numerous articles on education, training and occupational stratification and is the co-author of *The Problem of Sociology* (Hutchinson) and *Scheming for Youth* (Open University Press).

Malcolm Maguire is a Research Fellow in the Labour Market Studies Group at the University of Leicester. After graduating from Hull University he worked on a number of research projects in the field of youth, training and labour markets. He has published widely on the topic of youth employment and is co-author of a number of research papers and books, the latest being *Restructuring the Labour Market* (Macmillan).

Lydia Morris is a Lecturer in the Department of Sociology at the University of Essex. She is the author of *Household Finance Management and the Labour Market* (Avebury) and *The Workings of the Household* (Polity Press).

Mike Oliver is Reader in Disability Studies at Thames Polytechnic and was previously Lecturer in Social Work and Disability at the University of Kent and a Development Officer with Kent Spinal Services. He has been a tetraplegic since 1962 and is on the Examination and Management Committee of the Spinal Injuries Association and is also active in the disability movement. His previous books include *Social Work with Disabled People* (Macmillan) and *The Politics of Disablement* (Macmillan).

Richard Scase is Professor of Sociology at the University of Kent at Canterbury. He is the author of *Social Democracy in Capitalist Society* (1977) and co-author (with Robert Goffee) of *The Entrepreneurial Middle Class* (1982), *Women in Charge* (1985), *The Real World of the Small Business Owner* (1987), and *Reluctant Managers* (1989); and (with Howard Davis) of *Western Capitalism and State Socialism* (1985). He has edited four volumes and written numerous papers for academic and non-academic books and journals.

Robin Ward is Professor in Corporate Strategy at Trent Polytechnic and formerly Director of the Ethnic Business Research Unit at the University of Aston. His publications include numerous articles on ethnic business and, as editor, *Ethnic Communities in Business* (Cambridge University Press) and *Race and Residence in Britain* (ESRC). He has also recently edited a special issue on ethnic enterprise of the *International Small Business Journal* (vol. 4, 1986).

Preface

Many undergraduate courses in the social sciences, and particularly those in sociology, social administration and social policy, emphasize the ways whereby economic restructuring and government policies are having important ramifications for patterns of inequality and the dynamics of the class structure. It is often argued that labour markets are becoming increasingly polarized, divided and segmented with the effect that particular groups in society are experiencing various forms of deprivation, disadvantage and economic marginalization. It is suggested that new *social* divisions are emerging within Britain which, among other things, are leading to a polarization of the working class, with a substantial minority constituting an 'underclass' or, to put the case more precisely, a more clearly visible sub-stratum within the working class.

Many undergraduate courses within the social sciences – especially those that focus upon the changing structures of industrial societies – are devoting attention to these 'new' divisions and highlighting how the experiences of class are mediated through such factors as age, gender and ethnicity.

In any volume of this length it is impossible to cover all aspects of economic disadvantage as comprehensively as one would wish. This book does, however, aim to provide undergraduate students and other non-specialists with easy access to contemporary debates in a relatively simple and uncomplicated manner.

We make no apology for focusing on the economically and socially deprived in this volume. The contributors are aware that some people have 'never had it so good' but this is all the more reason why we should focus on those who have not. Indeed, we would argue that unless urgent steps are taken to ameliorate the social and economic conditions confronting the growing number of powerless and economically disadvantaged, it is society as a whole which will bear the consequences.

1

Social change and economic disadvantage in Britain

PHILLIP BROWN AND RICHARD SCASE

INTRODUCTION

Britain, during the past decade, has undergone a number of fundamental changes which some commentators have described as a social revolution. According to these, the institutional structure and its attendant ideologies have been transformed by a variety of economic, political and social forces such that little of 'the British way of life' has been untouched (Riddell, 1985; Gamble, 1988). Certainly, in comparison with the late 1970s, Britain of the 1990s is characterized by socio-economic features and prevailing ideological and political assumptions that are strikingly different. These changes, in their various ways, have had fundamental implications for class, gender and ethnic relations and, hence, for the distribution of socio-economic rewards and life chances. It is, then, only within these terms that the deprivations endured, and privileges enjoyed, by different groups in society can be fully understood.

The term that is most frequently used to summarize such changes is 'Thatcherism'. Hence, sociologists have been inclined to offer causal explanations by reference to the ascendancy of a political ideology in the 1980s which, so it is alleged, has had profound consequences for the social fabric of society (Hall and Jacques, 1983). We, however, are becoming dissatisfied with the nature of such explanatory accounts for at least two major reasons. First, notions of 'Thatcherism' are usually imprecise in both conceptual and empirical terms. In other words, it offers little in the form of operational specificities which can be hypothesized and tested on the basis of detailed and systematic empirical research. Second, even as a *causal* explanation, it is less than satisfactory since it detracts from the consideration of possibilities that Thatcherism as a socio-political phenomenon is, itself, the product of a variety of forces developing within British society in the 1970s

(Scase, 1989). At best, then, it is little more than a term of shorthand which may be used for summarizing the fundamental changes which have occurred in Britain during the past decade. What, then, are some of the more important of these?

Undoubtedly, the most fundamental are associated with different processes of economic restructuring. During the 1970s, it was increasingly recognized that the many sectors of industrial manufacturing were outdated, non-competitive and characterized by poor productivity and capital investment. Various strategies developed by governments – both Conservative and Labour – based upon corporatist assumptions, were seen to have failed to have brought about any significant improvements (Brittan, 1985). It was the election of the first Thatcher administration in 1979 which led to the pursuit of policies that were strikingly different to those of all previous post-war governments. The State was no longer to offer subsidies and forms of 'hidden' support to both private and public sector organizations. Instead, there was a return to 'market forces' with international and national competition determining the fate of major companies (Brittan, 1977). Such policies, coupled with high interest rates and a highly valued currency to curb inflation, had severe ramifications for the condition of manufacturing in Britain. Large sectors of export orientated engineering, shipbuilding and traditional heavy industry became unable to compete in world markets and this led to large-scale plant closures, redundancies and dramatic increases in overall levels of unemployment.

If these changes have, in part, been brought about by Conservative government policies, they have been reinforced by broader global developments. There has been the rapid industrialization of the Pacific rim with the production of manufactured goods that directly compete with those which traditionally have been produced in Britain. The availability of comparatively cheap labour and the absence of effective trade unions in these countries have made them favourable sites for economic production. Indeed, if these are the 'pull factors', there are also those which have 'pushed' production to these countries because of high levels of labour organization, expensive employment costs associated with social insurance, holiday and sickness benefits, and 'poor' industrial relations of the sort that characterize Western industrialized countries in general and Britain in particular. There has, then, been the emergence of a more evident international division of labour as far as the production of manufactured goods is concerned. This has brought about a tendency for high volume standardized products which use cheap labour inputs to be assembled in the less developed countries, while more high quality, complex and specialist products are made in Japan and in the more advanced Western countries.

If such global developments can be seen to be partly a result of corporate attempts to maintain competitive cost effectiveness through circumventing the challenges of organized labour in Britain and other Western countries, such a strategy has been further pursued through the automation and robotization of work processes (Forester, 1987). Hence, manufacturing processes are often characterized by low staffing levels with those workers retained undertaking either a variety of tasks within a less specified division of labour or, alternatively, providing various support or maintenance functions (Buchanan and McCalman, 1989). If, then, the nature of work within manufacturing corporations has changed, so too has the character of labour unionism and shop-floor organization. Indeed, these coupled as they are with broader technological developments and processes of economic restructuring, have had severe ramifications for class relations and for the position of the industrial working class. These, in turn, have affected the role of the labour movement, the Labour Party and the extent to which they are able to develop credible industrial and political policies.

If, however, there has been a reduction in the need for industrial manual employees, the work experiences of those now required are becoming rather different to those encountered during the earlier post-war decades. A number of writers use the notion of 'Post-Fordism' to describe trends in industrial production which are transcending more traditional forms of economic organization (Sabel, 1982). Throughout the twentieth century, the principles of 'Fordism' and the ideas of F. W. Taylor and Scientific Management have provided the underlying assumptions of management practice (Braverman, 1974). Accordingly, there has been an emphasis upon developing productive processes that capitalize upon the economies of scale. The emergence of mass markets since the 1920s has led to the growth of corporations which produce high volume goods, standardized in both quality and quantity. The automobile industry epitomizes most of these. Hence, the term Fordism – with its emphasis upon productive techniques within which there is the routinization of work tasks, a precisely-delineated division of labour, and the performance of operative duties that requires employees to exercise only the most rudimentary levels of discretion, judgement and skill. Thus, the development of assembly-line production methods, have brought about a general process of deskilling whereby productive workers have become subordinated to close managerial control which is exercised through the technological process (Braverman, 1974). Indeed, the growth of Fordist factory methods have separated the functional tasks of management and workers. While the former have become increasingly responsible for all aspects of planning, design and supervision, the latter are now little more than appendages to highly-complex, managerially-controlled technological processes. Thus, the twentieth century has witnessed the concentration of economic production within large-scale, corporations within which 'de-skilled' employees are engaged to perform routine and repetitive tasks on a relatively long-term basis. Indeed, the continuous development of such forms of production have been nurtured by the on-going expansion of mass markets and their demand for products manufactured according to these principles.

However, since the 1970s, many traditional Fordist assumptions have been questioned and many of the ideals of Scientific Management are becoming superseded by 'alternative' paradigms which claim that profit maximization can be achieved more effectively through 'flexible', decentralized and often, small-scale work processes (Atkinson, 1984a). A number of factors have contributed to this, but some of the more important are related to changes in the nature of markets, employer–employee relationships and consumer expectations.

If, in the immediate post-war decades, there was relative stability in market growth – despite demand fluctuations associated with government policies and economic cycles – world markets are now characterized by a greater degree of uncertainty, with the industrialization of South-East Asian countries, competitive pressures have become more acute and profit margins less predictable. Product cycles have become shorter and there is now a greater need for companies to constantly innovate and trade with new products and services in order to survive. Corporations are now compelled to be more adaptive or 'flexible' in their production techniques and instead of producing relatively long runs of standardized goods, they are now forced to produce commodities for more specialized market niches (Atkinson, 1984b). Indeed, this is a strategy which is being increasingly adopted by large Western corporations. In order to compete with the high-volume low-cost producers in developing countries – with many of their production methods continuing to be based upon Fordist principles – Western Corporations are manufacturing more specialist, 'quality' products, targeted to the needs of specific market groups. This means that work activities must be managed so that operatives – instead of undertaking routinized tasks within a highly developed, detailed division of labour – are recruited as all-round general labourers who are able to exercise a limited degree of discretion and judgement within the context of work teams. These highly limited responsibilities are nurtured according to management principles variously described as JIT (Just In Time), HPWS (High Performance Work Systems), TQM (Total Quality Management) and QCs (Quality Circles) (Buchanan and McCalman, 1989). With the implementation of these principles, the more rigorous ideals of Scientific Management are abandoned and there are positive attempts to breakdown the more rigid boundaries that have traditionally existed between management and workers. If, according to Fordist principles, the functions of 'conception' and 'execution' (Braverman, 1974) must be separated and allocated as the respective tasks of management and workers, 'flexible' or 'Post-Fordist' methods attempt to reduce this divide: not at the level of strategic decision-making, but in terms of day-to-day operational issues.

Such a development has been encouraged by the need to establish more harmonious industrial relations. Factories organized according to Fordist criteria tend to foster worker–manager conflict if only because of the inherent social relations of such enterprises (Fox, 1974). The performance of routinized, deskilled work tasks within large-scale productive units encourages job dissatisfaction and an essentially instrumental orientation to work. They offer favourable circumstances for the growth of trade unionism, strong shop-floor organization and the development of various forms of collective solidarity. Often this will spill over into the development of broader socio-political activities that foster strong attachments to broader, class-based labour movements. The development of flexible production methods, however, offers managers strategies whereby these forces can be countered. By abandoning some of the more extreme dimensions of the detailed division of labour and by attempting to 'integrate' workers within lower-level management decision making and by creating a strong company culture, it is likely that a greater level of worker commitment to corporate goals can be achieved (Wickens, 1987). Equally, the organization of production on the basis of short runs, often within smaller de-centralized units, requiring the use of more general worker skills, is likely to reduce shop-floor solidarity and hence, conditions under which trade unionism and collective consciousness are likely to grow.

The transition to such methods of production are further being encouraged by changes in consumer preferences and expectations. If, as in the past, there continue to be mass markets for standardized, high volume goods, these are becoming supplemented by more specialized demands. The higher earnings enjoyed by the middle classes of Western societies have given them more disposable income to spend on various 'luxury' goods of one kind or another. This has enabled 'fashions' and 'trends' to be stimulated which, in turn, has led to a demand for more specialized goods and services. Equally, the desire for 'self-expression' and 'personal authenticity' has generated market needs for more 'personalized' life-styles (Scase and Goffee, 1987). Taken together, these patterns provide market niches for low volume, quality goods which offer high profit margins to both manufacturers and distributors. Hence, there is the need for flexible production methods which can quickly adapt from the manufacture of one product to another. Often this means that the goods produced consist of a number of 'core' elements upon which 'differences' in, for instance, colour, design, size, etc. are grafted in order to meet the more specialist demands of various market niches. Automobile, textile or furniture manufacturing plants are perhaps the best-known examples of such production methods.

Taken together, changes in market conditions, management strategies to improve industrial relations and the growth of consumer 'niches' for more specialist products, have brought about the need for more adaptive, flexible production processes. Although these enable managerial profit-making goals to be achieved, there are associated costs which are overwhelmingly borne by those engaged in different working-class occupations. Instead of employees being engaged on a relatively permanent basis, enjoying legislative protection in terms of health and safety, employment and general working conditions, they are now likely to be more exposed to the vagaries of the labour market. Thus, the *reality* of the 'flexible' firm is the use of part-time and casual employees as well as the subcontracting out of work tasks to those who are either fiscally self-employed or running their own small businesses

(Handy, 1984). Equally, the production of commodities and the delivery of services are often undertaken through a variety of franchising and sub-contracting arrangements, the majority of which enable manufacturers and retailers to reduce their risks, to keep overheads low and to optimize their profit margins. For those with only their labour to offer in the market, the outcome of such developments is not only greater uncertainty in their working lives, but greater vulnerability to periods of under-employment or unemployment. Further, if they are employed in small businesses who are acting as franchises or subcontractors for larger corporations, they are likely to be poorly paid and relatively disadvantaged in terms of their employment and working conditions (Gerry, 1985). Accordingly, the development of more flexible productive and distributive systems – expressed as these are in different forms of corporate restructuring, are having important ramifications for the material living and working conditions of many sectors of the working class. Indeed, such processes are bringing about a restructuring of class relationships, to say nothing of the ways in which these are affecting the character and composition of the working class in terms of its occupational groupings; age, gender and ethnic categories; and its collective expression through organized labour and trade unionism. We now turn our attention to some of the more detailed trends as these are affecting the rewards, opportunities and life-styles of those in working-class positions.

THE CHANGING PATTERN OF WORK AND EMPLOYMENT

Over the last century there have been significant quantitative and qualitative changes in work and employment. In particular we have witnessed the decline in primary sector employment such as agriculture, construction and mining and secondary sector employment in manufacturing, but a sizable increase in the proportion of people working in the service sector (distribution, catering, banking, business services, etc.). The number of people working in manufacturing industries between 1971 and 1988 declined by almost 3 million, from a little over 8 million to approximately 5 million. During the same period the numbers working in service industries increased by approximately 3.5 million from 11.6 million to 15.2 million (Central Statistical Office, 1989).

As a result of these changes there has been a substantial shift from skilled and semi-skilled manual jobs to non-manual employment (see Table 1.1). This shift towards technical, professional and managerial employment is set to continue as is the decline in semi- and unskilled manual jobs (Rajin and Pearson, 1986; Allen and Massey, 1988). One possible interpretation of these findings is that the kinds of jobs people do now are more interesting and knowledge based than was previously the case. There is certainly evidence to

Table 1.1. Distribution (per cent) of the economically active population by occupational category: Great Britain 1951–1981

	1951	1961	1971	1981
Employers and own account	6.7	6.4	6.5	6.4
Managers and administrators	5.4	5.3	8.0	10.1
Professionals and technicians	6.6	9.0	11.1	14.7
Clerical and sales	16.3	18.6	19.5	19.3
Supervisors and foremen	2.6	2.9	3.9	4.2
Skilled manual	23.8	24.1	20.2	16.0
Semi-skilled manual	26.6	25.1	19.3	19.0
Unskilled manual	11.9	8.5	11.6	10.4
Total	99.0	99.9	100.1	100.1
N (thousands)	22.514	23.639	25.021	25.406

Source: Heath and McDonald, 1987; reprinted in Sarre (1989).

support the view that there is a greater demand for expert labour and that some jobs have increased in their skill content. However, as we have already noted, this cannot be understood as a universal phenomenon. The 'service sector' includes many jobs which are poorly paid, insecure, part-time and usually performed by women. In 1988, 82 per cent of women were employed in the service sector and approximately two-thirds of these were in just four types of jobs: catering, cleaning, hairdressing and clerical work. What is more, the proportion of female employees has increased substantially from a quarter of those in paid employment in 1901 to 43 per cent in 1988. The entire increase of the labour force by 1.8 million between 1971–1986 can be accounted for by the increase in the number of women in the labour force (Central Statistical Office, 1988; Gallie, 1988), while the number of males in employment has declined over the last decade. In Chapter 7 Harris shows that it is especially older male workers who have had to bear the brunt of redundancy and to cope with an often unwelcome extension to their period of retirement dependent upon state benefits and often inadequate employment pensions. However, although more females are in employment, this expansion has been largely a result of the rapid increase in part-time work.

There has also been an increase in the number of self-employed. In 1988 the self-employed accounted for 12 per cent of the workforce in employment compared to 8 per cent in 1971 (Central Statistical Office, 1989). The Conservative government has presented this increase as a manifestation of changing social attitudes and an expression of the entrepreneurial spirit. But researchers have pointed out that the more likely cause of the increase in self-employment has been the response to unemployment and changes in employer policy, where employers concerned about reducing overheads have encouraged their staff to become self-employed. These people then continue to carry out the same type of work as before but under a different employment contract (Rubery, 1988, p. 267).

The increasing use of part-time female workers and the expansion of the self-employed and those on short-term contracts has been used to support the argument that there is a dual labour force of 'core' workers with secure and high waged jobs and 'peripheral' workers in insecure and low waged work (Dex, 1985; Allen and Massey, 1988). It is argued that this has provided employers with 'numerical flexibility' which will allow them to reduce labour costs and respond quickly to changing and uncertain market conditions. The argument about 'numerical flexibility' is examined by Ralph Favre in Chapter 4, who is led to doubt its empirical applicability on a large scale.

Whether there is convincing empirical evidence of an increasing polariz-ation between 'core' and 'peripheral' workers must remain an open question, although there would seem to be a significant minority of jobs which can be characterized as 'poor work'. However, the polarization debates should not stop at the factory gates or office door. We are not only concerned about those in jobs but also with the sizeable minority who are economically active in the sense that they want jobs but are unable to find one. Moreover, much of the *work* undertaken by women is for the household and hence unwaged.

This broader definition of work stems from a recognition that work is undertaken within as well as outside of the household, and that the material conditions of individual members of a household depend upon the economic activity of more than one member, traditionally regarded as the male breadwinner. The increased importance attached to the household has also led to a recognition that the lack of waged employment is not only an individual problem but a family affair having implications for all its members (Harris, 1987).

In the last twenty years we have witnessed an exponential increase in the numbers unemployed and those whose unemployment has been long-term (over one year). Unemployment has been a major political issue for much of the last decade throughout Western Europe. The UK has suffered one of the highest unemployment rates among Organization for European Co-operation and Development (OECD) countries, although official rates of unemployment in the UK have declined from 12.4 per cent in 1983 to 8.3 per cent in 1988 (see Ashton and Maguire, Chapter 3).

There is little doubt that this decline is in part a consequence of new job opportunities and the declining numbers of school leavers who are now entering the labour market. Nevertheless, the proportions officially defined as unemployed substantially underestimate the proportions unemployed given the Conservative Government's attempt to massage the figures in numerous ways (Marsh, 1988). There are also important regional differences in unemployment rates within the UK. Northern Ireland has traditionally had the highest rate of unemployment (17.9 per cent) and although this is higher than the North of England, there is evidence of a North/South divide. There were 6.5 per cent unemployed in the South East in 1988 compared to 14.1 per

cent in the North. The availability of employment obviously has consequences for the material well-being of the household. It is therefore not surprising to find that there are significant regional variations in the amount of
disposable income. In 1987 (using a £ per head index – UK = 100), the
index for the North of England was 91, the West Midlands was 89.6,
Greater London was 126.4 and the South East was 115.8 (Economic
Trends, 1988).

There is also a growing literature on the individual and household
consequences of unemployment. This literature shows that the household
consequences of unemployment depend upon its duration. Long-term
unemployment (over one year) accounted for 41 per cent of unemployed
males in 1989 and 29.5 per cent of females. The population of females
experiencing long-term unemployment as reported in official statistics is
particularly misleading because many married women cease signing on at an
unemployment office after one year because they exhaust their entitlement
to benefit.

The more optimistic interpretations of the consequences of unemployment pointed to an expanding 'informal' or 'hidden' economy which offered
work and financial rewards despite the fact that these jobs and the income
they derived do not 'officially' exist. It was also suggested that long-term
unemployment amongst men, and the attendant increase in female economic activity rates, generated the possibility of greater gender equality as a
result of 'role reversal'. Women would become the breadwinners and the
husbands would perform domestic household duties. The subsequent empirical evidence has generated little support for either hypothesis. The research by Pahl and Wallace (1985) revealed a situation contrary to earlier
expectations. Rather than the unemployed being able to mitigate the problems associated with unemployment through informal work, they found
that formal activity breeds informal activity. It was those in employment
who were also found to engage in a whole range of informal work both
inside and outside of the household. Without the money earned from formal
employment the unemployed were excluded from these activities as much as
waged employment and this led Pahl and Wallace to conclude:

> Therefore employment status is the key to participation in all forms of
> work, not simply that in the formal economy. Put negatively, un-
> employed men are more likely to be in households doing little self-
> provisioning and doing little or no informal work outside the house-
> hold themselves. Hence, there is a process of *polarisation* between the
> busy, highly work motivated households, generally well-off with mul-
> tiple earners and potential household workers, and others who are at
> the opposite end of the scale. (p. 378)

Research evidence concerning 'role-reversal' arrives at much the same
conclusion, that unemployed husbands are more likely to have unemployed

wives. Lydia Morris (Chapter 5) explains why the impact of male unemployment has led to a reinforcement of gender divisions, both inside and outside
the household, rather than being a social harbinger of sexual equality.

The bulk of the research evidence which has addressed the problems of
unemployment has drawn the conclusion that its solution depends upon
access to waged employment, and the consequence of its absence for a large
minority is a growing polarization of the British population between the
'haves' and 'have-nots'.

A popular interpretation of the social polarization thesis is to perceive the
unemployed as part of an 'underclass' in British society, for instance, Field
(1989) suggests that 'the recruiting sergeant has been active in the ranks of the
long-term unemployed' (p. 4). Field also argues that Britain's underclass is
also drawn from the ranks of single-parent families and the very old (p. 24).
In 1970, for example, the number of single-parent families drawing
supplementary benefit stood at 191 000. However, this number has significantly increased since 1979, up to 644 000 by May 1987 (Field, 1989, p. 25).
The number of old people has increased in recent years, which is making this
population increasingly dependent upon occupational and state pensions.
Without an adequate occupational pension to supplement their state pension
it is virtually impossible for old people to participate fully in the social life of
the surrounding neighbourhood. One only has to think about the reported
deaths from hypothermia, which follow periods of cold weather due to a lack
of adequate heating, to recognize that a significant minority of old people
suffer the same deprivation as the long-term unemployed and some
single-parent families. We certainly agree with Field that there are a growing
proportion of the population who are trapped in poverty, and that the state is
doing little to support the poor and to identify those who are 'losing out'. We
do not, however, subscribe to the notion of an 'underclass' for reasons which
will become clear in the contribution from Hartley Dean. One of the major
problems with the notion of an underclass is that it becomes a caricature of
social life which leads to the neat division between 'us', the majority of
responsible and respectable citizens, and 'them', the dependent and often
feckless minority who contribute little to the neighbourhoods in which they
live. Once we can separate out social groups in this way, there is a propensity
to 'blame the victim' for their circumstances, even by writers like Field who
would clearly not subscribe to such a view. This often takes the form of a
cultural explanation, for those on the left the 'culture of poverty' is a
consequence of structural inequalities, and for those on the right it is the cause
of poverty. Once the problems associated with multiple deprivation are
defined in these terms the cause and effect become rather like the chicken and
the egg, and arguments about the need to end the culture of dependence by
generating a culture of enterprise become almost irresistible especially to
right-wing politicians.

There is little empirical evidence to support the assertion that among the
disparate groups of the unemployed, old and single-parent families there is a

distinctive set of subcultural values and attitudes which set them apart from the rest of society. What they share is a life of poverty. What the empirical evidence has consistently highlighted is the enduring commitment to find employment, to fulfil social responsibilities, and to lead a dignified life. The change in the life-styles of the vast majority of long-term unemployed, for example, are not brought about as a result of apostasy but a pragmatic response to make ends meet. Moreover, the social and material conditions of those who experience multiple deprivation are not substantially different from a much larger section of the population, who may be in waged work but poorly paid.

There is a close relationship between social class and multiple deprivation (Rentoul, 1987; Hudson and Williams, 1989). Yet the idea of an 'underclass' implies that an understanding of the social and material conditions of this group is beyond class analysis. What is more plausible than the idea of an emerging 'underclass' is the view that British society has become increasingly polarized. In conclusion of their empirical study of social divisions within contemporary British society Hudson and Williams conclude:

> It has been demonstrated . . . that UK society has become more deeply divided since 1979 as a result of Thatcherite policies. Moreover, the growing divisions are a deliberate rather than an inadvertent conse-quence of those policies. In claiming this, we do not deny that prior to 1979 there were already deep divisions in UK society. Nor do we wish to suggest that existing inequalities have simply been widened. Rather, the dimensions of division have been selectively reworked, redefined *and* magnified at one and the same time. Divisions by class, gender, race and space are more pronounced than they were in 1979 but at the same time the pattern of inequalities has been altered. (p. 216)

Much of the empirical evidence supports this conclusion but the increasing inequalities are not simply a product of central government policy, as we have already suggested, but of longer term changes in the structure of the economy and the labour market (Pond, 1989, p. 55). Nevertheless as Pond has noted:

> Although the public presentation of government policy in the Thatcher years was that the role of the state was to intervene as little as possible in redistribution, in fact taxation, social security and labour market policy all result in a substantial redistribution of income and wealth, albeit in a direction previously considered unacceptable. (p. 65)

In other words, the wealthy and those in professional and managerial jobs are receiving an increasing share of Britain's material resources while those who are in 'poor work' or unemployed are having to survive on a declining proportion of material and consumer goods and services.

To some, this conclusion may appear surprising given the general increase in the standard of living and the increase in the number of people who own their homes and own shares. The proportion of the population owning shares between 1983 and 1987 rose from 5 per cent to 23 per cent, and it has become more evenly spread across socio-economic groups (Hudson and Williams, p. 39). Much of this change has resulted from the privatization of state assets and is reflected in the fact that over three-quarters of those who own shares have shares in only one or two companies. Therefore, 'popular capitalism' has done little to alter the general shift toward institutional share holding and the concentration of power and wealth in the hands of a small number of individuals and families.

The scale of economic inequalities in the 1980s, which are usually measured in terms of income and wealth, are difficult to assess due to a lack of data. The 1979 Conservative Government axed The Royal Commission on the Distribution of Income and Wealth which could have generated invaluable information. On the basis of what data are available it does appear that there has been some modest redistribution of wealth, but it has been among the wealthy rather than a general redistribution. As Pond has noted:

> There is a remarkable symmetry about wealth inequalities in the 1980s: while ten per cent of the population own more than half the nation's wealth, half the population own less than ten per cent. (op. cit., p. 69)

As a source of personal wealth the rises in house prices and the sale of council houses has been far more significant than share ownership resulting from the privatization of state assets. This is reflected in the fact that in 1971 dwellings accounted for 22.1 per cent of personal wealth and in 1987 this proportion increased to 33.0 per cent. The proportions for stocks and shares were 21.7 and 10.3 per cent respectively (Central Statistical Office, 1989).

The distribution of income presents a clear picture of the extent and growth of inequalities in Britain in the 1980s. Table 1.2 shows that the bottom fifth of wage earners in 1986 was less than half of one per cent while the top fifth of earners have increased their percentage share of income from 44 per cent in 1975 to 51 per cent in 1986.

After taxation and the payment of cash benefits the bottom quintile received 6.2 per cent of disposable income in 1975 and this declined to 5.1 per cent in 1986. These figures do not include the additional tax concessions following subsequent government legislation, and the 'community charge' (poll tax) which have substantially favoured those on high incomes. Therefore the proportion of disposable income of the top quintile which increased from 39 per cent to 45 per cent between 1975 and 1986 is likely to increase further and primarily at the expense of the low earners.

The main benefactors of 'free market' policies have, therefore, been those who were already relatively privileged. This is reflected not only in the reduction of the top rate of taxation from 83 to 40 per cent, but also favourable share options for executives which allowed Sir Ralph Halpern, Chairperson of the Burton Group, to exercise his share options and make an additional profit of £1.6 million independent of his usual salary, which

Table 1.2. Percentage shares of original income and income after cash benefits and all taxes

Quintile Group	1975	1986
Original income		
Bottom	0.8	0.3
2nd	10	6
3rd	19	16
4th	26	27
Top	44	51
Income after cash benefits and all taxes		
Bottom	6.2	5.1
2nd	12	10
3rd	18	16
4th	24	24
Top	39	45

Source: Economic Trends No.422, December 1988, Central Statistical Office.

in 1988 was £1 359 000 per annum (see Hudson and Williams, 1989). Against the policies which have benefited the high income earners must be stacked those policies aimed at low earners and the unemployed. The Thatcher Governments have attempted to reduce state expenditure on social welfare and drive down wages to price the unemployed back into jobs. This has happened at a time when fewer workers are protected by trade union membership; the wages councils, which had the power to lay down minimum rates of pay, have been dismantled, and the government has initiated a number of programmes for the young and unemployed which encourage employers to take on workers at low rates of pay (see Field, Chapter 2). Despite such attempts to reduce state expenditure the number claiming supplementary benefit increased from 1.2 to nearly 3.2 million between 1979 and 1989 (excluding pensioners). Therefore, even the more conservative estimates of those living on or below the poverty line now register approximately 8.2 million receiving supplementary benefit in 1988.

So far we have argued that there is evidence of an increasing social and economic polarization in Britain in the range of opportunities for waged work and in the rewards such employment offers. This is not to deny that an increasing number of jobs will require more knowledge and skills for their performance, but this does not render obsolete the bulk of 'poor work'. The increase in economic inequalities which have resulted from high rates of unemployment and increasing wage differentials have not only divided the population materially (in terms of the life-styles different social groups are able to purchase) but has also increased the requirement for certification and training which are increasingly demanded of those in 'core' employment, given that it is these jobs which offer good salaries and interesting work opportunities. The ideological justification for these inequalities include the need to encourage individual enterprise and reward talent. Basic to such justifications is the assertion that everyone starts off with an equal opportunity to achieve the best jobs. The pervasive power of the ideology of equality of opportunity continues to exert itself, despite the available empirical evidence which shows that those in the higher socio-economic categories (e.g. managers, accountants, administrators, employers) not only enjoy relatively privileged life-styles themselves, but have a much better chance, compared with those in routine semi and unskilled jobs, of reproducing the same advantages for their children. Therefore economic inequalities tend to be reproduced from generation to generation, and the polarization we have noted above seems set to increase social divisions, particularly as the better off invest some of their newly acquired wealth and income on private health care and education.

THE DISTRIBUTION OF WORK AND DISADVANTAGE

The burden of poor work and social disadvantage is not evenly distributed. Social class, gender, race and region are all of importance, as are age and disability. For the purpose of analysis, it is obviously important to examine each of these variables separately, but this should not obscure the fact that class, gender and race are interrelated, for example, if your parents are from the Afro-Caribbean they are more likely to be in low paid employment. If you are a white middle-class woman your life chances and life-style are likely to be substantially different from a black working-class woman (see Ward and Cross, Chapter 8).

Within a capitalist society it is hardly surprising that a large number of social researchers locate the *class structure* at the centre of their analysis, although there is considerable disagreement about what constitutes class and where one should draw the line between different 'classes' (Parkin, 1979). Although these issues are of considerable significance, they need not concern us here because however we define class and wherever we mark the boundary between different social groups, there are important differences, quite literally, in the chances and quality of life. In 1971 the death rate for adult men in unskilled work was nearly twice that of adult men in professional jobs, even when account had been taken of the different age structures of the two socio-economic groups (Field, 1989, p. 58). During the period 1979–1983 it has become more difficult to obtain adequate information, but a report in the *British Medical Journal* (August, 1986) concluded that 'The mortality rate of men higher up in the social scale has improved, and that of those lower down

Table 1.3. Social class of United Kingdom candidates accepted for Universities (percentages), 1979–1984

Social class	Percentage accepted	
	1979	*1984*
Professional, managerial, technical occupations	19.8	22.1
Intermediate occupations	38.0	48.2
Skilled occupations, non-manual	21.1	10.1
Skilled occupations, manual	14.7	12.4
Partly skilled occupations	4.5	6.2
Unskilled occupations	0.9	2.1

Source: Hudson and Williams, 1989, p. 62.

the scale has deteriorated' (in Field, p. 63; Townsend, 1982). Such differences in health are not only a reflection of the quality of work undertaken by different social groups, but also the quality of life and environment in which these social groups live. These inequalities have consequences for the social, physical and intellectual development of their children, which can be seriously impaired when living in conditions of poverty. Equally, the privileged material conditions of the middle class permit a greater chance of obtaining schooling and academic credentials which are of increasing importance to secure good jobs. Table 1.3 shows the percentage accepted for universities according to social class.

Table 1.3 shows that approximately 70 per cent of candidates accepted for university entrance were from backgrounds where the father was in a professional, managerial, or technical occupation. The table also shows that the children from these backgrounds increased as a proportion of entrance between 1979 and 1984, whilst students whose fathers worked in skilled manual or routine non-manual jobs declined from 14.7 to 12.4 per cent, and 21.1 and 10.1 per cent respectively. Recent changes in educational policy are likely to extend these inequalities even further, as more of the costs of studying for a degree will have to be met by the individual student, which is likely to inhibit talented students from less affluent social backgrounds from undertaking additional study at more advanced levels. The government's commitment to the 'free market' which has encouraged more parents to send their children to private (independent) schools, and for schools to 'opt out' of the system of comprehensive education, also seems set to perpetrate inequalities in the access to the qualifications necessary to gain entry to higher education and good jobs (Brown, 1990).

This bedrock of unequal educational opportunities is bolstered rather than reshaped by the vocational training available to school leavers (and unemployed adults). Finegold and Sockice (1988) suggest that industrial training in Britain can be characterized in terms of a 'low-skill equilibrium':

> The best way to visualize this argument is to see Britain as trapped in a low-skills equilibrium, in which the majority of enterprises staffed by poorly trained managers and workers produce low-quality goods and services. The term 'equilibrium' is used to connote a self-reinforcing network of societal and state institutions which interact to stifle the demand for improvements in skill levels. This set of political-economic institutions will be shown to include: the organization of industry, firms and the work process, the industrial relations system, financial markets, the state and political structure, as well as the operation of the ET system. A change in any one of these factors without corresponding shifts in the other institutional variables may result in only small long-term shifts in the equilibrium position. For example, a company which decides to recruit better-educated workers and then invest more funds in training them will not realize the full potential of that investment if it does not make parallel changes in style and quality of management, work design, promotion structure and the way it implements new technologies. The same logic applies on a national scale to a state which invests in improving its ET system, while ignoring the surrounding industrial structure. (p. 22)

Chapter 6 by Lee confirms this view and in comparison to the training available to young workers in Germany, suggests that British youth are receiving an inferior preparation for working life and in the Single European Market they will be both technically and linguistically at a disadvantage. Moreover, despite all the rhetoric propounding the need for a better trained workforce, estimates from Labour Force surveys indicate that there was *less* job-related training for employees aged 16–19-years-old in 1987 than in 1985. In 1985, 29.3 per cent of males and 18.7 per cent of females between the ages of 16–19 were in job-related training, compared to 25.5 and 17.3 per cent respectively in 1987 (Central Statistical Office, 1989). These surveys also highlight clear gender divisions in the quality of training available to young women and men, and there is a considerable body of evidence to suggest that the kind of training received is also segregated according to gender (Cockburn, 1987). Inequalities in education and training have obvious implications for access to the labour market and for chances of obtaining good or poor work.

In recent years sociologists have been more interested in the operation of the labour market. The research evidence indicates that employers frequently use two different kinds of selection criteria: suitability and acceptability:

> Suitability is functionally specific, in as much as it is concerned with the individual's ability to perform the tasks required by the job. Criteria of

Table 1.4. Unemployment rates by ethnic group and qualifications, 1985–1987

	Great Britain		Percentage
	With qualifications	No qualifications	All
White	14	15	11
West Indian	24	22	21
Indian	15	21	16
Pakistani/Bangladeshi	29	32	29
Other	19	20	17

Source: Table 4.26, Social Trends, 1989, p. 81, Central Statistical Office.

suitability might include physique, particular experience or formal education, trade or professional qualifications. Acceptability is functionally non-specific, concerned with the general control and management of the organisation: will the recruit 'fit in' to the context in question, is he or she 'dependable', 'reliable' and hard working, will the new worker leave after a short time? Criteria of acceptability are highly subjective and dependent upon managerial perceptions, including appearance, 'manner and attitude', 'maturity', gender, 'labour market history', and age and marital status. (Jenkins, 1985, p. 319–20)

The selection criteria adopted by employers contributes to the manufacture of disadvantage in the competition for jobs. This has important implications for those with disabilities as Oliver clearly demonstrates in Chapter 9. Equally, Table 1.4 shows that both qualified and unqualified whites were more likely to be in employment than those from ethnic minorities. The nature and implications of racial divisions in employment are explained by Ward and Cross in Chapter 8.

The conclusion to be drawn from this brief review, and the more detailed discussions in subsequent chapters, is that there are significant divisions in the quality of work (even for those who are in employment), and also significant inequalities in access to employment on the basis of disability, age and region as well as social background, gender and race. What is perhaps most disturbing about this review is the fact that the divisions and inequalities we have examined appear to have increased during the 1980s as a result of economic change both nationally and globally, and as a result of central government policies. Whether these patterns will continue to the end of the 20th century is a matter of conjecture. But governmental or state-determined strategies are now widely considered to be inappropriate in confronting these socio-economic issues. It is a brief review of such changes upon which we now focus.

THE DEMISE OF CORPORATISM AND THE CHANGING POLITICAL AGENDA

In the 1970s much was written about the growing ascendancy of corporatism in Britain (Middlemas, 1979). By this was meant that both *macro* and *micro* economic management was determined by collaborative agreements between the representatives of capital, labour and the state. This, it was often argued, was functional for efficiency in circumstances where there was an increasing concentration of economic production within a very limited number of large-scale capitalist corporations. While, at the same time, the growth of trade unionism – brought about by these same trends – was increasing the economic and political influence of labour. Further, alongside such developments, was the growth of the state, not only in terms of its provision of health, welfare and education services but also through its increased intervention in regulating the economy. Concerns about inflation, regional imbalances, the urban fabric, housing and transport, to say nothing of the need to modernize and rationalize manufacturing led to its increasing involvement in industrial development and corporate change. Indeed, these *macro* developments had important ramifications at the *micro* or organizational level. As a result of 'negotiated settlements' between post-war governments and trade union leaders, legislation was introduced which aimed to regulate health and safety at work, employment security, equal opportunities for men and women, dismissal procedures, wage negotiations and so on. In other words, the managerial prerogatives became more constrained through the implementation of legislation and collective bargaining agreements (Crouch, 1979).

It was for these reasons that a number of political commentators, writing during the closing years of the 1970s, argued that Britain was no longer a market or capitalist economy and, as a consequence, political and trade union influences were determining the direction of economic management rather than market-based competition, profits and economic efficiency (Brittan, 1977). Indeed, fears of state socialism were frequently expressed, while it was often claimed that the growth of corporatist structures and the associated emergence of a 'strong state' were destroying individual freedoms (Crozier, 1979). Managers, so it was argued, had lost the right to manage, corporations were becoming increasingly subject to the dictates of trade union leaders, while citizens were losing a number of cherished choices because of state policies towards education, health and welfare. The ideals of corporatism were so ascendant in the 1970s that the parameters of discourse were seen to be becoming more constrained as ideas of *collectivism* superseded those of *individualism*. Accordingly, the growth of corporatism was perceived to be a growing threat to the traditional fabric of British society if only because it was seen to offer so few benefits. Irrespective of achievements in such areas as town and country planning, regional development, employment, housing, education and health, there was a growing perception that the British economy was failing, at least by international standards, and that political life was ideologically bankrupt. Indeed, such a perception was not the exclusive pressure of the political right. If there were observers of the 'new right' who warned of the perils of state corporatism, there were others of the left who, equally, argued of its dangers. For the latter, it represented a system of economic and political controls which operated to *incorporate* the interests of labour within the structure of monopoly capitalism (Panitch, 1980). As such, corporatism constituted a form of 'compromise' between the opposing classes of capital and labour which served the interests of the former through regulating the growing influence of the latter. For some writers of the left, therefore, corporatism constituted a functional requirement of monopoly capital. How, then, do these writers account for developments in Britain since the late 1970s?

Certainly, many corporatist structures have been dismantled as the state has withdrawn from involvement in direct economic planning, regional development, labour-management relations and the ownership of profit-making corporations. But, coupled with these institutional changes, there has been the emergence of a political culture which is the antithesis of the ideals and assumptions of earlier post-war decades. The parameter of public discourse has altered as 'new right' ideologies have emerged, emphasizing the desirability of market relations, entrepreneurship, private wealth creation and individualism. Residents in old people's homes have become 'customers' while managers of social service departments are trained to *market* their products in *cost-effective* and *profitable* ways. There has, in other words, been a transformation of prevailing assumptions within the public sector as well as in the privately-owned economy. Accordingly, there are few who are able to insulate themselves, let alone protect against these market-orientated political ideals.

There is, however, a belief among some commentators that the demise of corporatism and the ascendancy of 'free market' principles during the past decade is little more than either a temporary fashion or an aberration of the political process that will soon be corrected (McCrone, Elliott and Bechhofer, 1989). Equally, the rhetoric of private wealth creation, entrepreneurship and 'self-help' are of marginal importance which will have only limited longer-term implications. As a result, the analyses of new right ideologies and policies have received less attention than they deserve. Many social scientists in hoping for a return to orderly corporatism which, it is usually assumed, will be re-instated by an elected Labour government, have devoted little attention to the enterprise culture and the extent to which its ideals are affecting the strategies and styles of management in state-owned health, welfare and educational institutions (Burrows, 1990). Moreover, events in Eastern Europe raise fundamental questions about viable socialist alternatives to the 'free market' in the 1990s, and socio-political developments in Britain during the past decade have rendered obsolete – certainly for the foreseeable future – many of the prevailing assumptions and paradigms which shaped social science enquiry in the 1970s. Academic observers have often failed to address themselves to many of the fundamental changes which have occurred. In a sense, the same can be said of the Labour Party. Unlike its counterpart in many other European countries, it has been unable to formulate an agenda for political action which is derived from *contemporary* socio-economic conditions rather than from those steeped in the corporatist post-war decades. It has difficulty in accepting that state ownership of the means of production is *not* a popular issue and that the provision of collective services through *centralized* state agencies is interpreted by large sectors of society as potentially 'despotic' in its nature. Indeed, working-class experiences as claimants for social welfare, health and educational services of one kind or another frequently reaffirm their dependency, subordination and powerlessness in society. Instead of the welfare state enhancing individual choices and freedoms, the outcome for many has been the reaffirmation of their disadvantage and subjection. It is important not to fall into the rightist 'trap' on this but to emphasize that it is not the provision of state welfare services *per se* which requires scrutiny since they are a fundamental right of citizenship. Rather, it is to query their organization and provision on the basis of centralist, Fordist, bureaucratic principles. So far, the organization and provision of the civic activities of the state in Britain have been such that they have fuelled the ideologies of the New Right. By contrast, political commentators of the Left have largely failed to confront some of these shortcomings and as a consequence the development of credible strategies for state reform remain in their infancy (Brown and Sparks, 1989; Hall and Jacques, 1989). In the 1990s this is now even more difficult if only because of the changes which have occurred in Eastern Europe have globally weakened the legitimacy of state institutions.

It is, then, counterproductive for the Left in Britain to search for political strategies which are steeped in corporatist assumptions and which rest upon an extended state apparatus to tackle the fundamental economic and social problems facing Britain in the 1990s. Obviously, these cannot be confronted without a reformist government using the state machinery as an *agency* of political action. However, the institutional structures which are created will need to be somewhat different to those set up by earlier post-war Labour governments. Politics will need to recognize that there is, in the 1990s, a popular reaction against state collectivism. Citizens are now more concerned with their own personal autonomy and independence as a result, the institutional arrangements whereby their health, welfare and educational needs are met need to be structured accordingly. In short, the 1990s will witness a continuing shift towards 'post-Fordism' principles and the Labour Party will need to recognize these changes and to develop a compatible programme of social and economic reforms if it is to obtain the necessary electoral support to become a government. By contrast, the Social Democratic regimes in Scandinavia have responded rather more positively to these popular expectations and this is reflected in the extent to which they are 'de-bureaucratizing' and 'decentralizing' the state provision of various health, welfare and housing services. Traditional assumptions of democratic socialism are under review so that programmes of political action can respond to, and incorporate, the changing aspirations of both the 'new' and 'traditional' sectors of the working class. If, in the past, the appeals of trade unionism, collectivism and working-class solidarism have been sufficient to mobilize popular support, this is no longer considered to be the case. Social Democratic and Labour Party appeals – if they are to obtain widespread electoral support – must be compatible with the structural and ideological changes which have occurred within the working classes of different Western societies.

Because the terminology of 'personal freedoms' and 'individual choices' have been captured by the New Right they are often considered as values which are incompatible with state welfare systems (Harris, 1989). Supporters of the Labour Party are often reluctant to use such terms because of their contemporary political connotations. Again, political developments in Scandinavia suggest that this need not be the case. In Sweden, for instance, the Social Democratic Party argues for the need to expand state welfare provision on the very grounds that it *enhances* individual freedoms and choices. It refutes the antithesis of the 'individual' and the 'state' and, instead, argues that personal development and self-realization can only *substantively* be enjoyed by the greater majority of the population if the state underwrites their general material, social and psychological well-being. Without this, fundamental individual choices and freedoms remain the privilege of a small minority in society. Witness, for instance, the advantages enjoyed by those in Britain who are able to subscribe to private health insurance schemes and to afford preferential educational opportunities for their offspring.

If in Britain in the past, the production of goods within large-scale integrated technological processes sustained high levels of union density and along with this, loyalties to a working-class political movement, this seems unlikely to continue in the future. The decline of traditional industries such as coal mining, ship building and heavy engineering has had fundamental ramifications for the electoral support, to say nothing of the ideological appeals, of the Labour Party. Within the context of a more socially and economically divided society, geographically segmented by regional differences as well as by spatial differences within large cities, there appears to be no coherent political appeal which is able to express the aspirations and frustrations of those who are economically deprived and politically subordinated. The restructuring of class relationships have increased material inequalities but reduced the level of subjective awareness of them. Inequalities, privileges and disadvantages are now more likely to be viewed as the outcome of *individual* actions rather than of structurally-determined economic and political forces. A strongly nurtured dominant ideology of *individualism* has reinforced a prevailing culture of *indifference* which serves to sustain both the privileges and deprivations experienced by different groups in society. One of the most urgent issues to be tackled is the growing social and economic divide between what Therborn (1989) has described as the 'Two Thirds, One Third Society', by which he is referring to the fact that as much as one-third of the British population are becoming increasingly marginalized in poor regions, with poor resources, poor housing and poor work.

2

In search of the underclass

HARTLEY DEAN

> ... the changes made in the scope of welfare provision since 1979 ...
> amount to a mini-revolution, and have played a part in creating an
> underclass. (Field, 1989, p. 90)

> ... while the Government claims that it is targeting help on those in
> greatest need, it is simultaneously increasing the numbers caught, in the
> Government's terminology, in a 'dependency culture'. (ibid, p. 131)

This belief, expressed by Frank Field, veteran poverty campaigner and
Labour MP, typifies an increasingly popular view that, during the 1980s, a
new 'underclass' has emerged in Britain. An underclass separated in terms of
income, life chances and political aspirations from the mass of the population
as welfare benefit levels fail to keep pace with changes in earnings and as the
labour market and the very basis of citizenship are subjected to radical
restructuring.

Just as changes in social and economic policy are argued by some to have
contributed to the creation of an underclass, so the government for its part
rails against the cultural values ascribed to that underclass. In a widely
reported speech in 1987, John Moore, then Secretary of State for Health and
Social Security, condemned the 'dependency culture' of welfare benefit
recipients, contrasting it with the 'enterprise culture' of those who seek to
create wealth and opportunity. The paradox is concisely summed up by
Brown and Sparks (1989):

> It is an inherent feature of Thatcherism to protest against social trends
> which are of its own making. (p. xiv)

At the level of political discourse, Thatcherism has sought to blame its
victims by constructing the pejorative notion of 'dependency culture', while

the opponents of Thatcherism have sought to blame government policy by constructing a socio-structural notion of 'underclass'. The two notions are mirror images of the same discursive construct and each serves to feed and to taint the other.

SOCIAL POLARIZATION AND POVERTY

Whatever the cause, the British population has in recent years experienced an increase in economic inequality. Between 1976 and 1985 the percentage share of original incomes of the poorest fifth of households decreased by 63 per cent, while the share of the richest fifth increased by 10 per cent. Even allowing for the redistributive effects of social security benefits and taxation, the percentage share of final incomes of the poorest fifth still declined by 9 per cent while the share of the richest fifth still increased by 6 per cent (Byrne, 1987). In relative terms, the rich have got richer and the poor have got poorer, as illustrated by Brown and Scase in Chapter 1.

But have the poor got poorer in absolute terms? Between 1979 and 1985 there was a 55 per cent increase in the number of persons dependent upon Supplementary Benefit or living on incomes below or equivalent to the Supplementary Benefit level and there was a 33 per cent increase in the number of persons living on incomes below or equivalent to 140 per cent of the Supplementary Benefit level – whom the Child Poverty Action Group (CPAG) would define as living 'in or on the margins of poverty' (Oppenheim, 1988, p. 9). The DHSS attributed 50 per cent of this increase to a rise in the real value of Supplementary Benefit over that period but, as CPAG point out, 'Even if this view is accepted, the fact remains that the remaining 50 per cent of the increase is a rise in absolute poverty' (ibid, p. 8).

This 'fact' was vigorously contested in 1988 in another ministerial speech by the above mentioned John Moore, who protested that Supplementary Benefit or Income Support levels no longer provide a sensible measure of poverty in the UK and that the general rise in living standards in the 1980s signalled 'the end of the line for poverty'. The European Commission, however, whose Statistical Office have been working to establish a common European Poverty Line, have calculated that between 1975 and 1985, poverty in the UK more than doubled from 3 to 6.5 million – or 12 per cent of the population. In 1975, Britain suffered less poverty than nations such as Belgium, Germany or Italy, but by 1985 poverty in those countries was lower than in the UK, standing at 7.2, 8.5 and 11.7 per cent respectively (Brown, 1989).

What is more, the biggest single factor contributing to the increase in poverty has been the rise in unemployment. The proportion of unemployed persons amongst those with incomes below or equivalent to 140 per cent of Supplementary Benefit levels more than doubled between 1979 and 1985 – from 10 to 24 per cent (Oppenheim, 1988, p. 7). If the gap between rich and poor or between employed and unemployed has got wider, does this justify characterizing the poor or the unemployed as an underclass? Is it meaningful to define this underclass as being behaviourally or culturally deviant?

This chapter will contend that the poor and the unemployed are not a class in any analytical sense and that it is relations of power, fashioned through and by the modern state, which constitute poverty and unemployment as deviant and which turn 'dependency' into a cultural 'problem'.

DELINQUENCY, DEPENDENCY AND THE UNDERCLASS

The concept of 'underclass', as Macnicol has observed, has a 'long and undistinguished pedigree' (1987, p. 315) and, in various guises and at various times, it has been popular both in Britain and the USA. It is a concept which, empirically speaking, is hopelessly imprecise. And, as a theoretical device, it is a concept which has repeatedly conflated structural and cultural definitions of not only poverty, but of crime as well. It is a concept which seems periodically to be forged at points where structural and cultural explanations conflict.

The ultra-conservative American political scientist, Charles Murray, recently visited Britain to see to what extent the underclass 'disease' was spreading. He concluded that:

> Britain has a growing population of working-aged, healthy people who live in a different world from other Britons, who are raising their children to live in it, and whose values are now contaminating the life of entire neighbourhoods (Murray, 1989, p. 27).

But, responding to the question 'How big is Britain's underclass?', he conceded:

> It all depends on how one defines its membership; trying to take a head count is a waste of time. The size of the underclass can be made to look huge or insignificant, depending on what one wants the answer to be (ibid, p. 37).

For Murray, the phenomena which best predict 'an underclass in the making' are illegitimacy, violent crime, and drop out from the labour force. It is through his perception of an underclass that he is able to posit an interrelationship between such disparate phenomena. Potentially, the underclass can be as extensive as one's preoccupations with what does or doesn't constitute deviant behaviour.

'Underclass' is therefore a potent term which can capture popular fears and concerns regarding delinquency on the one hand and dependency on the other. Delinquency and dependency, however they may be explained, are perceived as inherently dangerous phenomena because, as Liebow (1967) put it:

> the one threatens the property, peace and good order of society at large; the other drains its purse. (p. 6)

I shall argue that the underclass concept is most interesting, not for its explanatory value, but for the way in which it has so often drawn together and illuminated preoccupations with delinquency and dependency and for the way in which it permits often unspoken associations between the two.

Michel Foucault (1977), in his celebrated account of the prison, attempted to deconstruct the term 'delinquency' arguing that, as a particular form of illegality, 'delinquency' is not necessarily the most socially harmful; it is merely the form against which penal policy and the penal apparatus are directed. Delinquency is thus:

> an effect of penality ... that makes it possible to differentiate, accommodate and supervise illegalities. (p. 276)

It is not that the penal system has thus far failed to eliminate crime, on the contrary, says Foucault, it has:

> succeeded extremely well in producing delinquency, as a specific type, a politically or economically less dangerous ... form of illegality; in producing delinquents in an apparently marginal, but in fact centrally supervised milieu; in producing the delinquent as a pathological subject. (p. 277)

I have argued in a similar vein that 'poverty' may be seen as an 'effect' of social security and relief systems (Dean, 1990, chp. 4): that poverty is a particular form of material deprivation that is sustained and rendered manageable through the very policy mechanisms calculated to prevent or relieve it. There is a danger, however, of glossing over the diversity of the discursive formulations which constitute the notion of 'poverty' and I shall here consider 'dependency' rather than 'poverty' (just as Foucault considered 'delinquency' rather than 'crime' or 'deviance').

Nineteenth-century Benthamite social commentators insisted (in terms not dissimilar from modern Thatcherites) that poverty was no more than the natural and necessary condition of free labour, whereas the true social evil was 'indigence' (i.e. dependency). The nineteenth century English Poor Law was therefore quite explicitly directed, not against poverty, but against 'pauperism', a status of dependency which poor relief set out simultaneously to define and to punish.

Nevertheless, whenever 'poverty' is rediscovered as a socio-structural 'problem' – such as in England in the latter part of the nineteenth century and in both the USA and the UK in the latter part of the twentieth century – so it seems are notions of 'residuum' or 'underclass' reinvented: all embracing notions which conveniently fudge socio-structural definition with cultural caricature and thus seek to address discursively constituted threats of dependency and delinquency as if they were objective social phenomena.

Thus in England (and especially London) in the latter part of the nineteenth century there arose an image and indeed a fear of 'a minority of the still unregenerate poor' (Stedman-Jones, 1971, p. 11):

> This group was variously referred to as 'the dangerous class', the casual poor or more characteristically, as the 'residuum'. (ibid)

Stedman-Jones suggests that a preoccupation with the 'residuum' was universal in conservative, liberal and socialist thought alike and that it stemmed from a fear that the 'residuum' might contaminate the 'respectable working class' or that it might even expand to such proportions as to envelop it.

I shall argue that the impetus to define a 'residuum' or 'underclass' has always stemmed from a concern to defend other assumptions concerning the integrity of existing social relations of production and reproduction and, in particular, of labour and the family. Proponents of the underclass concept have never been able satisfactorily to define or locate the members of their underclass other than by reference to the variety of afflictions or shortcomings which they supposedly exhibit (whether such afflictions be real or imagined, or the shortcomings culpable or innocent). In effect, the underclass is always negatively defined, not by criteria peculiar to the underclass, but by criteria of productive work and/or family life from which, for any number of reasons, the 'residuum' or 'underclass' is excluded. What is defined is not a class, but a residue; a stratum existing under or beneath the norms of class.

Even Marx and Engels (1970), when defining the 'lumpenproletariat', spoke of ' "the dangerous class", the social scum, that passively rotting mass thrown off by the lowest layers of old society' and were primarily concerned lest this underclass might not be drawn into the wider proletarian movement but become instead a 'bribed tool of reactionary intrigue' (p. 25). The dilemma facing the British Labour Party in the 1990s is seen by Field as one of how to build support amongst the mass of better off voters for policies which would 'spring' his posited underclass from its current position (1979, p. 156). The underclass, even if it is not actually a threat, is perceived as a potential impediment upon labour and the labour movement.

It is instructive therefore to consider the notions of 'residuum' and the 'underclass' as a discursive rather than objective phenomena, since they furnish a commentary upon the broader social relations which they have helped and are still helping to constitute.

THE HISTORY OF A DISCOURSE

Like all underclasses, the 'residuum' of Victorian England was ostensibly regarded by its various proponents in different ways. At one extreme, the hard liners of the Charity Organisation Society, dedicated to decreasing 'not suffering but sin' (Henrietta Barnett – quoted in Stedman-Jones, 1971, p. 271), viewed the problem of the residuum as a consequence of 'demoraliz-ation'. At the other extreme, new liberals and socialists, influenced by secular and social Darwinist ideas, began to explain the residuum more in terms of a theory of 'degeneration' (Stedman-Jones, 1971).

Henry Mayhew (1861), a journalist and champion of the downtrodden, had encompassed within his definition of the 'non-working' class three very disparate groups: those with physical defects, those with mental or intellec-tual defects (the 'lunatics and idiots') and those with moral defects (such as 'the vagrant, the professional mendicant and the criminal'). This taxonomy of defects was founded on a general belief that:

> while he (Mayhew) wishes to arouse the public to the social necessity of enabling every person throughout the kingdom to live in comfort by his labour, (he) has no wish to teach the humbler classes that they can possibly obtain a livelihood by any other means. (from correspondence; quoted in Stedman-Jones, 1971, p. 267)

Similarly, the pioneer social investigator, Charles Booth, who had demonstrated to his own alarm that in the 1880s 35 per cent of the population of Tower Hamlets was 'at all times more or less in want' (Booth, 1887, p. 375), was careful to distinguish the 'residuum' as but a relatively small group within the ranks of the poor – making up he estimated only 8.4 per cent of the total population in 1891 (Booth, 1902, vol. 2, p. 21). Booth divided the 'residuum' into two sub-classes. Class 'A', whom he described as 'loafers' or as 'the vicious and semi-criminal', he estimated to comprise less than 2 per cent of the East London population. Class 'B', whom he regarded as merely 'feckless' improvident and beyond self improvement, was a larger group whose membership tended inevitably to overlap with Class 'C' ('irregular earners') (Booth, 1902, vol. 1). Booth is by convention remem-bered as an opponent of the rigid doctrines of the Charity Organisation Society and as an advocate of 'limited socialism', with state pensions for the 'respectable' working class, but just as central to his prescription was the proposal that Classes 'A' and 'B', the 'residuum', should be dispersed out of London to labour colonies:

> To the rich the very poor are a sentimental interest. *To the poor they are a crushing load.* The poverty of the poor is mainly the result of the competition of the very poor. The entire removal of this very poor class out of the daily struggle for existence I believe to be the only solution to the problem. [emphasis added] (p. 154)

In spite of competing diagnoses and prescriptions, there appears in Victorian England to have been something amounting to a consensus that the 'problem' had more to do with protecting the integrity and aspirations of the 'respectable' working class and the 'honest' poor than it did with the afflictions of the residuum itself.

The ground for America's discovery of an 'underclass' in the 1980s was it seems laid some 20 years before when the USA had rediscovered poverty (see Harrington, 1962). A component part of the common wisdom which had informed 1960s liberalism at the time of President Johnson's 'War on Poverty' was an implicit or explicit acceptance of the 'culture of poverty' thesis, popularly ascribed to the anthropologist, Oscar Lewis.

Whereas Charles Booth had applied moral criteria in order to make a purportedly empirical distinction between a minority 'residuum' and 'the poor', so Lewis (1968) applied purportedly objective 'cultural' criteria so as to conclude that at:

> a rough guess . . . about 20% of the population below the poverty line . . . in the United States have characteristics which would justify classifying their way of life as a culture of poverty. (p. 57)

The term 'culture', according to Lewis (1965), implied 'a design for living which is passed down from generation to generation' (p. xxiv) and he claimed to have observed:

> remarkable similarities in family structure, interpersonal relations, time orientations, value systems, spending patterns, and the sense of community in lower class settlements in London, Glasgow, Paris, Harlem and Mexico City. (ibid)

Such cultural patterns, Lewis claimed, were transmitted from generation to generation so as to reinforce a recurring cycle of poverty. Whilst such a thesis could be called in aid of expanded relief programmes aimed at breaking such cycles of poverty, it also provided fuel for more conservative and eugenecist commentators who could now point to a hereditary dimension to poverty and a pathology not only of poor individuals, but of poor families. Indeed, a storm of controversy arose in 1965 when Daniel Moynihan, then Assistant Secretary of Labor, produced a White House report on the Negro family which concluded that 'the fundamental source of the weakness of the Negro community' was 'the deterioration of the Negro family'. Wilson (1987) claims that it was revulsion against the racist application of the culture of poverty thesis which deterred further interest in poverty matters on the part of the liberal academic community and which effectively deferred the onset of a debate which has more recently emerged in the USA about the American 'underclass'.

Wilson (1987) defines the underclass as:

> that heterogeneous grouping of families and individuals who are outside the mainstream of the American occupational system. Included . . . are individuals who lack training and skills and either experience long-term unemployment or are not members of the labor force, individuals who are engaged in street crime and other forms of aberrant

behaviour, and families that experience long-term spells of poverty and/or welfare dependency. (p. 8)

This however is only one of several definitions and much argument and energy has been expended trying to determine the size or extent of the American underclass. Estimates, based on differing measures, vary widely – from less than 1 per cent of the population to more than 10 per cent (Dahrendorf, 1987, p. 4). In spite of this lack of agreement or precision, there is supposedly a body of evidence which 'is at the moment taken by all shades of opinion to indicate a real phenomenon' (Manning, 1989, p. 8).

The phenomenon, as may be seen from Wilson's definition, is constituted at the point where structural considerations concerning the American occupational system intersect with cultural considerations dealing with delinquency, dependency and the family. The American underclass finds itself as the focus of a social policy debate between those on the right who would abolish federal welfare and income support measures and those on the left who would expand or at least redirect them. Commentators such as Murray (1984) argue (just as John Moore has done in the UK) that welfare creates a dependency culture; it embodies a set of disincentives which undermine the labour market and the family. Against this view, commentators of the left and centre have demonstrated that the effect of welfare on labour supply has been overestimated and that the rising numbers of female-headed families (i.e. 'unsupported' mothers) is a demographic trend unrelated to welfare programmes (for a summary of this debate see Manning, 1989, p. 9).

However, the political and academic debate is grounded upon a set of 'common sense' assumptions about the nature of the problem which the underclass is supposed to represent; and upon general and diverse preoccupations, not only with poverty, but with very real and pressing issues, such as race, urban crime and the ghetto. Wacquant and Wilson (1989) speak of 'the inter-related set of phenomena captured by the term underclass' (p. 8). It is of course the plasticity of the term underclass and its ability to 'capture' a range of concerns which has made it so popular and which enabled a New York journalist, Ken Auletta, to first bring the term to prominence in the early 1980s.

Auletta (1982) played in a sense the role of a modern-day Mayhew. He concluded:

. . . for most of the 25 to 29 million Americans officially classified as poor, poverty is not a permanent condition . . . most of these people overcome poverty after a generation or two. There are no precise numbers on this, but an estimated 9 million Americans do not assimilate. They are the underclass. Generally speaking they can be grouped into four distinct categories: (a) the *passive poor*, usually long term welfare recipients; (b) the *hostile* street criminals who terrorize most cities, and who are often school dropouts and drug addicts; (c) the *hustlers*, who, like street criminals may not be poor and who earn their livelihood in an underground economy, but rarely commit violent crimes; (d) the *traumatized* drunks, drifters, homeless shopping bag ladies and released mental patients who frequently roam or collapse on city streets. (p. xvi)

Like Mayhew, Auletta maps out a taxonomy of defects which incorporates both the delinquent and the dependent and which constitutes 'both America's peril and shame' (p. xviii). Auletta none the less paints a sympathetic portrait of the underclass and voices support for programmes directed to providing opportunities and assistance to its members. Yet, claiming to be neither a conservative nor a liberal, he acknowledges that welfare does encourage dependency and the break up of families. The problem he says is that both sides of the social policy debate talk past each other:

> We could extricate ourselves from this rhetorical quagmire if we simply admitted what common sense rather than doctrine dictated: Both sides are right. (ibid: p. 306)

The rejoinder to this assertion must surely be that if 'common sense' can dictate that welfare recipients and street criminals are related parts of the same problem, then perhaps neither side can be right. The underclass debate has in fact cemented a consensus of belief, not about the nature of the threat, but about what it is that is supposedly threatened, namely the labour market and the family system.

BRITAIN'S EMERGING UNDERCLASS

The underclass debate in the USA, while coinciding with the advent of the Reagan era of welfare retrenchment, harked back in many respects to an earlier debate over the culture of poverty thesis. A broadly similar pattern may be detected in the UK, where the underclass debate has been awakened by critics of social polarization under Thatcherism, yet it resonates with a variant of the culture of poverty thesis originally proposed in the 1970s by Sir Keith Joseph when Secretary of State for Health and Social Services in the Heath government, who was later to become a close adviser and supporter of Margaret Thatcher.

Between 1972 and 1974, Joseph delivered a series of speeches in which he identified a phenomenon he called the 'cycle of deprivation'. Like Lewis, he claimed there was a process by which multiple deprivation and social disadvantage could be intergenerationally transmitted:

> Do we not know only too certainly that among the children of this generation there are some doomed to an uphill struggle against the disadvantages of a deprived family background? Do we not know that

many of them will not be able to overcome the disadvantages and will become in their turn the parents of deprived families? (Joseph, 1972)

Extensive research subsequently commissioned by the Department of Health and Social Security and the Social Science Research Council demonstrated nothing of the sort (see Brown and Madge, 1982): the intergenerational cycle of Joseph's popular imagination, if it could be said to exist at all, was in reality frequently broken by individuals and families alike. None the less, the seeds of a debate had been sown.

Peter Townsend, who condemned Joseph's cycle of deprivation thesis as 'a mixture of popular stereotypes and ill developed, mostly contentious scientific notions' (1974, p. 8), sought to explain the persistence and the patterns of deprivation in structural rather than cultural terms:

> A large, and proportionately increasing, section of the population are neither part of the paid workforce nor members of the households of that workforce . . . they have been denied access to paid employment, conceded incomes equivalent in value to bare subsistence, attracted specially defined low social status as minority groups, and accommodated, as a result, within the social structure as a kind of modern 'underclass'. (Townsend, 1979, p. 920)

Similarly, Bill Jordan (1974), while dismissive of Joseph's cultural thesis, had argued that those dependent on state income support had been assigned by the welfare state to a newly created underclass or 'claiming class' (Jordan, 1973).

While those on the right sought to identify a culturally distinct deprived minority, those on the left sought to identify a structurally defined underclass. The 'culturalists' were concerned with the 'problem family'; the 'structuralists' with 'poverty'.

The term 'underclass' was however only casually used during the 1970s and it was in the 1980s that the influential Ralph Dahrendorf brought it to centre stage, presenting the underclass as a 'cancer which eats away at the texture of societies and metastasizes in ways which can increasingly be felt in all their parts' (Dahrendorf, 1987, p. 3). Dahrendorf sought to concert the analysis of economic restructuring and demographic trends with ideas about culture and counter-culture, concluding that:

> something like a million British people are characterized by a syndrome of deprivation which often leads to a 'ghetto' existence. The syndrome is also a vicious circle. Once people have got into it, they find it hard to break out. They are not clinging on precariously to a 'normal' world of jobs and life chances, but settling into a life cycle of their own. This is sufficiently different from the rest to make them feel they have no stake in the official society. (p. 4)

Concern has been expressed that, in detecting new divisions in British society, proponents of the underclass thesis may be running ahead of the evidence (see Pahl, 1988, p. 258). But, evidence apart, the hypothesis advanced by Dahrendorf is in many ways wider than that taken on board in the American debate, because his concept of underclass is accompanied by a challenge to conventional assumptions about the future feasibility of full employment ['Work itself' he says 'is part of the problem' (1987, p. 9)] and about the adequacy of the protection of our modern rights of citizenship (which he claims are fundamentally violated by the existence of a powerless, disenfranchised underclass).

Yet, within the discourse of the hypothesis, is an implicit link between, on the one hand questions of state dependency and the limitations of the labour market, and on the other hand the non-compliance of the excluded with the norms of society: crime, says Dahrendorf, 'is one of the modes of life of the underclass' (ibid, p. 5). The possibility that the underclass might expand or harden is regarded as a threat to Britain's social and political stability and also to its 'moral hygiene' (ibid, p. 11).

It was within this climate that Frank Field (1989) introduced his own account of the emergence of Britain's underclass (to which I have already referred). Field's simplistic definition of the underclass has much in common with Jordan's 'claiming class' of the 1970s and encompasses three disparate groups: the long-term unemployed, single parents and elderly people without occupational pensions. The only thing which the three groups have in common is dependency on state benefits and, indeed, the tax and benefit systems are Field's central preoccupation. Field clearly demonstrates the scale upon which economic inequalities have widened during the 1980s, but his choice of the term 'underclass' appears to have been made primarily for dramatic effect. The almost gratuitous use of such a term is significant none the less. Field effectively sidesteps Dahrendorf's broader arguments by accepting that an underclass culture exists, but insisting that we should not blame victims but strive in the longer term to return to full employment and a fairer welfare state. Dependency culture is by implication accepted as a real phenomenon and the 'underclass' is admitted as a legitimate term in political and social policy discourse.

THE INFORMAL ECONOMY

A central and legitimate concern of social policy commentators, like Field, has been the effect of the unemployment and poverty 'traps' resulting from the interaction between low wage rates, the tax structure and means-tested benefit levels. Field (1989) argues that these traps operate heavily against the underclass and those at its margin and that:

> One way open to the individual to beat these two traps is to make dishonest returns to the tax office, the benefit office or both. Participation in the black economy [sic] may produce substantial short-term gains for the individual concerned, but these gains have to be offset

against the 'rights of citizenship' that go with a complete national insurance contributions record. Such exclusion from citizenship is again the mark of the underclass. (p. 131)

Here Field gives voice to a popular assumption which links the notion of underclass to the existence of a 'hidden' or 'informal' economy. If there was a distinct class of persons systematically engaged in illegal forms of economic activity, there is a sense in which it could legitimately be regarded as an 'underclass'. The evidence, however, suggests otherwise.

There are no reliable estimates of the size of the informal economy. Such estimates as are made are based, either on anecdotal evidence or on macro-economic measures of the discrepancies between reported income and expenditure measures of Gross Domestic Product. Such measures do not accurately identify the participants in the informal economy and, as Catherine Hakim (1988) points out, they are likely to include up to 5 million people whose activities are not in any respect illegal. Included in this figure are some 3 million regular workers whose earnings do not exceed the tax and/or National Insurance thresholds and some 2 million workers whose 'jobs' do not count as such in official statistics and whose earnings are too trivial to count for tax or welfare benefit purposes. Hakim suggests that speculation about the scale of an ill-defined informal economy has had a stigmatizing effect which reinforces distinctions – not between the employed and the unemployed – but between primary or 'core' workers in stable employment and secondary or 'peripheral' workers engaged in the expanding sphere of part-time, flexible, irregular or precarious forms of 'self-employment'.

Further light is cast upon the significance of the informal economy by Ray Pahl's research findings. Five per cent of the adults included in his study on Sheppey acknowledged doing work 'on your own account for extra money'. Of these one-third were housewives without regular employment and the remainder were working, rather than unemployed (Pahl, 1984). Pahl went on to observe that those doing informal work were likely to be members of households in which there was already one or more full-time workers (and/or to be full-time workers themselves). The opportunities for participating in the informal economy were greater for the members of already 'work rich' households than for 'work poor' households who usually lacked the material resources and/or the social contacts necessary for such participation. His argument is that employers' strategies and household work practices act in concert to compound the process of social polarization (Pahl, 1988).

The intersecting notions of 'informal economy' and 'underclass' are bound up with certain complex processes of social polarization, and may even fuel such processes. However, neither notion relates in practice to the other, in so far as the participants in the informal economy cannot justly be characterized as members of the underclass (or vice versa), and both notions arise from assumptions which are equally inexact.

DEPENDENCY AND THE SYMBOLISM OF THE UNDERCLASS

'Underclass' is a symbolic term with no single meaning, but a great many applications. It is used both in global descriptions of the exclusionary processes of class based societies and as an almost causal short-hand notation in debates about social and economic inequality. It represents, not a useful concept, but a potent symbol.

Foucault (1977) has argued that, as industrial capitalism matured, the physical means by which 'abnormal' individuals were segregated from the 'pure' community became generalized so as to function throughout society in accordance with a 'double mode':

> that of binary division and branding (mad/sane; dangerous/harmless; normal/abnormal); and that of coercive assignment, of differentiated distribution (who he is; where he must be; how he is to be characterized . . .). (p. 199)

If we are to construe this to imply, as Foucault does, that techniques once specific to penal or remedial establishments became inherent to power relations in general, then I would argue that the underclass (or residuum) is indeed *par excellence* a symbolic device for the division and branding of the delinquent and the dependent and for their assignment to a very particular social location, status and identity. The underclass is a symbolic rather than an actual institution, capable of serving at a discursive level as a repository for those whom society would segregate or exclude.

Foucault himself has analysed the division and branding of the 'delinquent'. What I am arguing is that, in the recurring debate about the underclass, we may also see the evidence of a related and parallel process – the division and branding of the 'dependent'.

The current debate about 'dependency' in relation to the underclass is thus oriented around the binary axis of work versus welfare. Independence implies the norm of the wage relation and the mutually self-sufficient family; dependency implies the 'abnormal' and, in particular, unemployment or single parenthood and the receipt of welfare benefits. Financial dependency on the state (rather than upon the wage or the family) is translated into a problem of behavioural dependency.

David Ellwood has recently reviewed and evaluated three models of behavioural dependency (1989): the rational choice model, which assumes that individuals will evaluate the options they face in accordance with 'tastes and preferences': expectancy models, which look upon dependency as the result of a loss of confidence or the loss by the individual of a sense of control over his/her life: and cultural models, which regard dependency as a behavioural deficiency and/or the consequence of aberrant social mores. Ellwood's broad conclusion was that, when seeking to explain the statistical patterns of long-term welfare dependency in the USA, it is the rational choice model which best fits the data in so far as the economic and marital options open to single mothers on long-term welfare posed unreasonable choices and could therefore reasonably explain their continued reliance on welfare. Ellwood was less convinced when it came to explaining the evidence of changing family structure patterns associated with welfare dependency in so far as individual choices in this sphere are more complex and less observable and that expectancy and cultural models, 'although capable of making widely divergent predictions with only modest variations in assumptions' (p. 13), may have relevance.

The assumption behind all three models, which goes unquestioned by Ellwood, is that long-term welfare dependency by single mothers is potentially problematic, both economically and for the 'traditional family'. The assumed policy objective is to guarantee that male breadwinners will earn and will marry and will be able to support child-bearing women and children. Ellwood concedes that 'Of course people with confidence and mainstream values form single-parent households' and that, according to current research, the typical child born in the US will spend at least some time in a single parent home. But, he insists:

> some behaviour – such as births to unmarried teenagers – is harder to understand and justify using a choice model, especially when the mothers are in no position to provide for themselves, much less their babies. (p. 12)

For Ellwood, therefore, welfare dependency remains problematic because it is not economically rational; it must sometimes be explained in terms of defective expectations and/or adverse cultural values. It was Auletta (1982), however, who explained unmarried teenage motherhood by quoting from conversations he had with members of the Little Sisters of the Assumption, a religious order in East Harlem running a surrogate mother programme:

> When they look into life, what do they see? It's not as if they were planning their life. Their life is planned in a sense . . . Maybe in one day the mother has to keep three appointments – food stamps, welfare, a clinic. Depending on these systems for survival creates a way of life whereby your life becomes more and more organized by the systems. And remember, these *are* systems of dependency. You can sense a taking away of the family by the system . . . 20% of the residential units here in East Harlem are vacant. An additional 10% are near aban-donment. So what do people look at when they wake up? They have no hope. What is within your ability? Becoming a mother. (quote, p. 71)

> A baby is something everyone considers something of worth. You don't have anything of value of your own. A baby is of value. People who are educated and work try to build something which lasts beyond them. Its the same for poor people. (quote p. 72)

The Little Sisters of the Assumption thus attribute an amoral form of rationality to welfare dependency. A rationality derived none the less from prevailing notions of what is to be valued; dependency that is displaced from the family to the system.

Similarly, for 18 – 24-year-old young people in the north east of England in 1987, amongst whom almost one in three had never had a full-time job (Observer, 25/1/87), the real choice even for the relatively well educated was between 'shit jobs, govvy schemes or the dole' (ESRC, 1987, p. 17). Research indicated that a clear majority of these youngsters were 'non-political, pragmatic young adults. . . eager for employment, even on modest wages' and 'far from advancing a rebellious morality, they were conservative on most social issues' (ibid). Although, upon such evidence, welfare dependency could not be regarded as irrational or aberrant behaviour, Leicester University's Labour Market Studies Group claimed to have found that:

> People who have to exist on social security have a different set of values. Morality starts to change. Small-scale thieving is seen as part of every day life. (Observer, 25/1/87)

The single mothers of East Harlem and the unemployed youngsters of North East England are all candidates for inclusion as members of a posited 'underclass', characterized not by their misfortune, their lack of rationality, nor even by distinctive cultural values or expectations, but by a failure of morality. Welfare dependency is suspect, it is an underclass phenomenon, because it seems to threaten what Dahrendorf referred to as our 'moral hygiene'; because it represents in fact an inversion of acceptable dependency.

Durkheim's (1964) classic thesis had been that, as the social division of labour increases and individuals become more specialized or differentiated, so do they become more socially dependent: the mutual interdependence that is characteristic of social existence becomes more complex. This in a sense was the starting point for the Fabian conception of welfare (Titmuss, 1963), whereby more and more:

> 'states of dependency' have been defined and recognised as collective responsibilities, and more differentiated provision has been made in respect of them. These 'states of dependency' arise for the vast majority of the population whenever they are not in a position to 'earn life' for themselves and their families; they are then dependent people. (p. 42)

Yet behind the notion of collective responsibility for dependent people remained an assumption in favour of individual responsibility on the part of wage earners and their families, whose dependency is surely no less 'social' merely because their dependency is mediated through the wage relation and the family, rather than through the state. Concealed beneath what Marx (1970) referred to as the 'dull compulsion' of the wage relation lie, not the 'free' labourers of bourgeois rhetoric, but individuals who are dependent upon the sale of their labour power for the means of their subsistence. And, for the reproduction of individual labour power, each individual is further dependent upon the socially determined structure of the modern nuclear family.

Ironically, therefore, those who are dependent on collective provision by an impersonal state have become *independent* of the wage relation and/or the family. Welfare dependents are not of course 'free', but are enmeshed and identified by state mechanisms of surveillance and discipline, just as delinquents are enmeshed and identified by state penalty. The common ground upon which dependents and delinquents can be symbolically assigned to an 'underclass' is that they each offend against norms which are peculiar to capitalist social relations and they are socially constituted through their respective relationships with state authority.

In his quest for an antidote to the 'underclass', Ken Auletta (1982) quotes with approval the sentiments of a highly charismatic 45-year-old black woman teacher running a Chicago ghetto school, who had been featured in a CBS television documentary:

> Even when the four-year-olds begin to read 'The Little Red Hen', I point out the moral, that if you don't work you don't eat. (quoted, p. 309)

But does this homily – 'if you don't work you don't eat' – represent a moral or a rational imperative? The abstract conclusion to be drawn from 'The Little Red Hen' is that people must contribute to the life of a community if they are to be sustained by it: anthropologically speaking, this amounts to a recognition of rational necessity. It is only because the wage relation (something specific to capitalist social relations) intervenes between the individual and the community and mediates their mutual interdependence that the homily takes on the character of a moral fetish. State welfare benefits and indeed crime can and do provide the means to eat without the necessity for waged work, but in each case the scope of the relationship between the individual and the community (and the potential for reciprocity) is strictly fashioned, regulated or embargoed through the intermediary of highly specific state institutions. At the level of discourse and popular common-sense, the creation of an underclass affirms rather than refutes the moral premise of 'The Little Red Hen'.

Writing before the term 'underclass' had been popularized in the USA, Liebow (1967) described in perceptive detail the life of 'Negro street corner men' in downtown Washington DC. What characterized and explained the behaviour of these men was their own perception of their own failures – as men, as workers, as fathers, as husbands and lovers. The poor paid and menial jobs which were in practice available to them did not satisfy their aspirations to reasonable pay and status. The fluidity and volatility evinced in their relationships with women and children did not satisfy their aspirations to be patriarchal providers. Street-corner life was essentially an accommo-dation to failure in terms of values, sentiments and beliefs shared with the 'larger society'. Liebow concluded that the inside world of the street-corner men (that which might now be referred to as 'underclass culture') did not in fact arise from, nor did it produce a distinctive counter-culture. On the contrary:

> It is in continuous, intimate contact with the larger society – indeed, it is an integral part of it – and is no more impervious to the values, sentiments and beliefs of the larger society than it is to the blue welfare checks or to the agents of the larger society, such as the policeman, the police informer, the case worker, the landlord, the dope pusher . . . (p. 209)

The 'underclass' is no more and no less than a symbolic manifestation of socially constituted definitions of failure. The term does not usefully define a real or tangible phenomenon, but inevitably it touches upon real and important issues, to do with work, the family and citizenship. Social commentators and policy makers would do well to avoid the term, but they must address the social divisions which generate or constitute the perceived 'failures' of the unemployed, the single parent and the welfare claimant.

Recent structural and cultural changes have intersected, not to produce an 'underclass', but to shift the boundaries between core workers, peripheral workers and non-workers; between the individual and the family; and between the citizen and the welfare state. Such changes have also exacerbated regional inequalities and inner-city decay and, some would argue, may have contributed to rising levels of crime. We should not go in search of the underclass, but strive for a better understanding of structural and cultural changes and their complex interrelationship and effects.

3
Patterns and experiences of unemployment

DAVID N. ASHTON AND MALCOLM MAGUIRE

INTRODUCTION: THE CAUSES OF UNEMPLOYMENT

To understand the problem of unemployment we must first locate the British experience in the international context. Britain has not been alone in experiencing high levels of unemployment for the last decade. This has led some to argue that high levels of unemployment are inevitable as Western industrial societies undergo a period of adjustment to the structural changes which occurred in the 1970s and 1980s. The nature of these changes is now well established in the literature. They include the spread of global markets and the reorganization of production in some industries on a world-wide basis, the relocation of the capital for labour intensive production to low labour cost countries, the widespread introduction of micro-electronic technology and the rapid growth of new jobs in the service sector. Such changes are seen by many to coincide with a new phase of economic development, or a new long wave of economic development.

Kondratiev identified what he described as long waves in economic development. These are economic cycles spanning periods of 50 years, the first 25 years of which are characterized by an upswing in which new industries and technologies are developed, leading to rapid growth and high levels of employment. This is followed by a 25 year downswing in which the potential of the new industries is exhausted and stagnation sets in, leading to a decline in employment levels. Many believe that the crisis of the 1980s represents the trough of the last long wave which started after the Second World War. The scale of the changes cited above would indicate that the 1980s have indeed been a period of major societal adjustments.

The question we must now answer is whether these changes are sufficient to explain why Britain has experienced such high levels of unemployment.

More precisely, do such economic changes provide an adequate explanation of the British experience? The answer is emphatically 'no'. Although economic factors play a part they do not fully explain the high levels of unemployment experienced in Britain and some other Western industrial societies.

Therborn (1986) has shown in his study of the causes of unemployment in 16 countries that five countries, namely Norway, Sweden, Austria, Japan and Switzerland, came through the depression of the early eighties with rates of unemployment of 4 per cent or less. Moreover, his study also indicated that the conventional explanations given for the persistence of high levels of unemployment are inaccurate. For example, he found that changes in both the rate of economic growth, which affects the speed at which jobs are created, and in the labour supply, which affects the number of people looking for work, accounted for relatively little of the differences in the levels of unemployment in the sixteen countries. Other factors, such as the dependence of the economy on world markets, explained even less of the variance, and changes in the level of inflation, explained none at all. Clearly, these conventional economic causes tell us very little about why the level of unemployment differs so markedly between societies. The answer, Therborn suggests, is in the extent to which there is a political commitment to the maintenance of full employment on the part of ruling elites. Of course, this is only the start of an explanation, because we are now left with the problem of why it is that some societies have institutionalized a political commitment to full employment, while others have not, and whether this explanation covers all the societies in question. What is evident is that we have to look well beyond conventional economic explanations if we are to understand the different national experiences.

We can conclude from this that the impact of the world recession was mediated by the policies of the individual nation states which it affected. Thus, although the establishment of global markets may have reduced the autonomy of individual nation states, they still retain sufficient independence to exert a powerful influence over the domestic level of unemployment. Some chose to let it rise, while others, such as Sweden and Norway, maintained full employment. Yet even when unemployment was allowed to rise, as in Britain, the Government's social and economic policies still had a dramatic impact on the structure of the labour market and on the distribution and experience of unemployment.

STRUCTURAL CHANGES

The extension of global markets and the subsequent organization of production on an international basis has a number of implications for the structure of labour markets. First, it has meant that in Britain many firms in the traditional manufacturing industries of textiles, footwear, engineering, shipbuilding, steel and metal manufacture either went out of business or changed their business strategy in response to intensified international competition. One-third of the manual jobs in engineering were lost during the period 1979–1984 and thousands more were lost in the footwear and textile industries as the capital necessary for manufacturing was relocated. The growth of the global markets and the relocation of capital preceded the recession but were accelerated by it.

In responding to these changes, jobs were lost in manufacturing which traditionally provided the occupational base of large sections of the working class. Many of the larger firms which survived the recession did so by adopting one of two courses of action. Some changed their business strategy by pulling out of those parts of the market where they could no longer compete with newly industrialized countries or low labour cost countries, and adopted a strategy of establishing market niches (Rubery, Tarling and Wilkinson, 1987). Others changed their labour market strategy to enable them to continue to compete in existing markets, usually by reducing the number of manufacturing units and making redundancies.

The pressure to restructure labour management came from the squeeze on labour costs and the growing awareness of alternative forms of labour management, particularly those developed by Japanese companies and some American-owned multinationals. These new labour management strategies were seen to be associated with the much higher levels of productivity necessary if British firms were to compete successfully in world markets. They offered management the prospect of much greater flexibility in their use of labour.

The strategies many firms tried to adopt involved offering a core of their workforce employment security in return for them adopting flexible working practices. This 'core' workforce was then supplemented by a 'peripheral' workforce comprising temporary, part-time, or sub-contracted workers, who offered another kind of flexibility, a numerical one, whereby firms were able to adjust the size of their workforce to fluctuations in the demand for the firm's product. The constituent elements of this strategy have been described in some detail in the work of the Institute of Manpower Studies (Atkinson, 1984b; NEDO, 1986), in the concept of the 'flexible firm'. The recent work of Ashton, Maguire and Spilsbury (1990) and the results of the 1987 ACAS survey (ACAS, 1988) suggest that there have been important changes in the ways in which firms organize their labour forces, especially among the larger firms. As a result of such changes some of the lines of demarcation which have separated the activities of members of traditional crafts such as electricians and fitters have been eroded, if not abolished. This process has tended to weaken the workers' sense of identification with their trades while managements have encouraged them to identify more closely with their firms. Companies have also sought to reduce the old status distinctions between white-collar and blue-collar staff, for example, by getting rid of separate canteen facilities and holiday entitlements which favoured the white-collar staff. As they struggled to enhance their competitiveness, firms reduced the size of their labour force and increasingly resorted to the use of casual, temporary and part-time workers to meet fluctuations in the demand for their products. These were the new 'flexible' workers (Lane, 1988). There is less commitment on the part of the firm to such workers as they can be hired and fired almost at will. Subcontracting work is another technique that is used to meet fluctuations in the demand for the firm's product. Thus, as the number of semi-skilled and skilled manual workers in relatively secure, full-time employment is reduced, the number of 'flexible' insecure workers is increased. This latter group are employed on fixed-term or part-time contracts in jobs which provide a very tenuous foothold in the labour market. However, just how far these changes have permeated remains a matter of some debate (Pollert, 1988a; Rubery, 1988).

Another feature of the companies which have survived is that they tend to be involved in those industries making sophisticated products which require heavy capital investment, for example, in the production of chemicals, computers and information technology. It is these industries where the Western industrial societies retain an advantage in global markets. In Britain, as elsewhere, such companies tend to concentrate geographically in areas where unions are relatively weak. This leads to imbalances in the demand for labour at the local level and helps create the large concentrations of long-term unemployed found in many inner-city areas and in many of the northern cities.

In their attempts to compete in international markets British companies have been forced to introduce new technology on a large scale during the recession (Gill, 1985). It is widely believed that this technology has contributed towards the eradication of many manual jobs in manufacturing, although it has proved difficult to separate the impact of technological change from other factors such as the effects of the recession. The introduction of new technology has also changed the relationship between employment and output in those industries, by offering the prospect of enhancing manufacturing output without significantly increasing the demand for labour. The full implications of this for the labour market are still a matter of some debate (Elgar, 1987), but it is now clear that this technology has reduced the amount of unskilled, semi-skilled and skilled manual labour necessary for the manufacturing process. This means that, even in those firms which remain, there will be few of the full-time manual jobs, which have traditionally formed the basis of the manual working class.

The weakness of organized labour, and the Government's trade union policies, provided the opportunity for management to move in the directions outlined above. As with all social change, the extent to which it has taken place varies both within and between different sections of manufacturing industry and there are still areas where it may not have penetrated. Trends in the service sector, notably in local government and the retail and leisure industries have a different source. What we are focusing upon, however, is the general direction of change and its constituent elements.

Companies in many parts of the service sector such as the retail, hotel and catering and leisure industries, continue to operate in what remain predominantly domestic product markets. The source of change here comes from the increasing concentration of control over these markets by the large corporations which are rapidly replacing the traditional family firm. For example, in the leisure industry, the travelling fair gives way to giant theme parks, the small independent betting shop to the corporate chain. Similarly, in the restaurant trade the family enterprise is swallowed up by the multiple enterprise, and in hotels the family hotel is replaced by a national chain. These large companies have a number of competitive advantages over the family firms and are gradually replacing them. By standardizing both the product and the quality of service for a nationwide market, they are able to achieve economies of scale which are denied to smaller operators. However, part of their competitive advantage is their more efficient use of labour. Unlike the manufacturing companies which still have a relatively large 'core' labour force, the service companies have a small core of professional managers but rely on the extensive use of part-time workers. As they replace the smaller independents, and as demand in these product markets expands, these part-time jobs are the ones which continue to grow. Once again many of these jobs provide only a tenuous foothold in the labour market, although some do provide secure employment (Gallie and Vogler, 1988).

The effects of these economic changes on the labour force have been reinforced, and in many instances accelerated, by changes in the political process. Throughout the Western world numerous governments have sought to introduce greater 'flexibility' into their labour markets as part of their general economic strategy (Rosenberg, 1989). In Britain the Thatcher administration has sought to introduce such policies across many areas of labour market intervention. These have included the initial attempts to reduce the demands of government bureaucracy on businesses, legislative changes aimed at weakening the bargaining power of trade unions, and attempts to reduce the security of workers which had previously been provided by employment protection legislation. By 1986 it was estimated that one-third of workers had lost former rights (Bryne, 1987). Together, the lifting of legal constraints on employers and the reduction of trade union power have combined to provide employers with greater freedom of action in pushing through changes in labour management practices.

The government has also sought to introduce a greater 'flexibility' into the labour market more directly by the use of its control of the public sector. Those areas which have not been privatized, such as the health service and local government, have been obliged to subcontract work through enforced competitive tendering and make substantial reductions in their staffing, often converting full-time jobs to part-time jobs in the process.

The other political tools used to create changes in the labour market have been the powers of taxation and the control over the welfare system. Direct taxation has been reduced to create 'an incentive to work' and 'to reward hard work'. On the other hand, low wages have been stimulated by the use of trainee allowances on government schemes and the abolition of the wages councils. In addition, through changes in the administration of welfare benefits, attempts have been made to encourage or, if necessary, coerce the unemployed into accepting any available job.

Across a range of areas the government has thus played a major part in restructuring the labour market. It has helped create the conditions in which management could introduce the changes it sought in conditions of work and working practices. By its actions in reducing public expenditure it has contributed to the increase in the number of part-time and insecure workers and by the introduction of schemes such as the Young Workers Scheme and the low level of the trainee allowance it paid to those on the Youth Training Scheme, it has helped drive down the relative earnings of some of the lower paid workers (Ashton, Maguire and Spilsbury, 1990).

CONSEQUENCES OF POLITICAL AND ECONOMIC CHANGE FOR THE STRUCTURE OF THE LABOUR MARKET

The result of these changes has been a continued expansion of the professional, administrative and scientific occupations but a major decline in 'middle-level' blue-collar jobs, while at the base of the hierarchy there has been the growth of a new group of part-time, insecure, low paid jobs. These trends are not confined to Britain; in North America similar developments have been described as the 'declining middle' thesis (Krahn and Lowe, 1988).

As a consequence there has been a significant change in the class structure. At the lower levels, the decline in employment in the manufacturing industries, allied to the effects of the introduction of new technology, has destroyed many of the jobs which formed the economic basis of the traditional male manual working class and which provided a way into the labour market for many job seekers from the ethnic minority communities. However, the growth of the service industries, and the rationalization of labour which has taken place there, has led to the creation of new semi-skilled and unskilled jobs and service sector jobs. A very large proportion of these, although by no means all, have been part-time casual and temporary (Gallie and Vogler, 1988), and the majority have been filled by women. Thus, the effects of these changes have been to transform both the type of lower level jobs available and the sex composition of the labour force.

NEW PATTERNS OF UNEMPLOYMENT

In previous downturns of the business cycle, during the 1950s, 1960s and 1970s the social composition of the unemployed changed in fairly predictable ways. At times of strong business confidence, when employers invested, creating new jobs and a relatively low level of unemployment, the unemployed consisted of the elderly, the sick and the unskilled. As the business cycle turned down and employers held back on investment, the level of unemployment rose and the above were joined by the young seeking entry to the labour market, the semi-skilled and some skilled workers, so that the social composition of the unemployed started to approximate more closely that of the employed population. An economic upturn, with a consequent reduction in unemployment levels led to the skilled workers being the first to return to employment, followed by other mature workers with skills until the social composition of the unemployed more closely resembled what it had previously been (Ashton, 1986).

Similar changes took place in the relationship between short-term and long-term unemployment. At the start of the downturn the numbers flowing into unemployment were greater than the outflow, so that the level of unemployment rose. However, at this stage the unemployed consisted primarily of the relatively short-term unemployed. As the level continued to rise, those with few skills found it increasingly difficult to compete for jobs, while those who had recently entered the ranks of the unemployed with marketable skills were the first to flow out into jobs. Thus, the proportion of long-term unemployed started to increase and even during an economic upturn, these were the last to leave the pool of the unemployed.

In the 1979–1984 recession significant deviations to this pattern occurred. First, many more youths entered the ranks of the unemployed than had been the case in the past. Young people leaving school found the routes into the labour market closed to them. When adult unemployment rises youth unemployment tends to rise to a disproportionately greater degree, but the magnitude of the last recession was such that whole cohorts of school-leavers were finding it almost impossible to get a job immediately on leaving school (Raffe, 1987). This mass youth unemployment made a significant contribution to the riots which took place in many cities during the summer of 1981. Secondly, many of the unemployed were relatively highly-skilled workers who were finding it increasingly difficult to find another job (White, 1983). In previous economic downturns, they had experienced little difficulty in moving out of the ranks of the unemployed. In fact, the jobs which were growing in numbers throughout the eighties were the part-time jobs, which adult male skilled workers were not seeking, and for which they were not deemed suitable by employers. Thirdly, unlike in previous recessions, as the economy recovered, the proportion of unemployed, especially of the long-term unemployed, continued to rise. Indeed, ten years after the start of the recession the level of unemployment remained almost a million above what it had been in 1979. A fourth difference was the growing concentration of the long-term unemployed in the inner cities and the old industrial towns of the Midlands and the North. A widening division emerged between the affluent, who were participating in the recovery, and the unemployed, who were increasingly being excluded from mainstream society. This division was somewhat imperfectly captured in the popular notion of the North/South divide. All this suggested that the experience of the 1980s was different from that of the past.

Research results have begun to reveal something of the nature of these differences. Studies of redundant workers (White, 1983; Harris, 1987) found that many of those who were forced to leave their jobs during the recession were not moving directly into the ranks of the long-term unemployed. Some were taking short-term jobs, others became self-employed, while yet others entered government training schemes. What was characteristic of almost all of them, including the self-employed, was that they typically had relatively short periods of employment, followed by further spells of unemployment. Harris found that many of the skilled workers were unable to obtain jobs commensurate with their previous skills and had to accept any work that was on offer. In effect, the available work was shared out among a larger number of people, so that when each period of employment finished there was often a lengthy spell of unemployment before the next short-term period of employment or government scheme became available. Harris refers to this as the 'chequered pattern'.

Research in the 1970s (Norris, 1978) had identified a similar pattern of work/unemployment experience and termed it sub-employment. However, this pattern was only found among the unskilled workers. What the research of the 1980s revealed was that this pattern was now much more widespread and no longer confined to the unskilled.

Studies of young adults in four contrasting local labour markets (Ashton and Maguire 1986; Ashton, Maguire and Spilsbury 1990), found a similar pattern of experience. Young adults who entered the labour market just before and during the recession found difficulty in securing any job, but once in the labour market those who entered the lower segments found themselves moving from government schemes to unskilled and semi-skilled jobs, before experiencing further periods of unemployment. For them the experience of unemployment was a 'normal' part of their labour market history. Just how long these spells of unemployment lasted depended on where they lived and the state of the local labour market. Moreover, of that sample of 18–24-year olds, 10 per cent had never experienced a full-time job since leaving school. Again the chances of this happening depended very much on where the young adult lived. For those who lived in the affluent areas of the South East, in this instance St Albans, where only 2 per cent of females and 3 per cent of males had failed to obtain a full-time paid job, their chances of obtaining employment were far greater than in the depressed area of Sunderland, where the corresponding figures were 26 and 31 per cent, respectively.

These and other results suggest that for young people as well as adults, what employment was available was shared out among a large number of people. Moreover, because many of the new opportunities were in either short-term or casual jobs or in training schemes of limited duration, there was a constant circulation of labour among them. In general this meant that the higher the level of unemployment in the locality, the longer people had to wait between jobs and the higher the proportion who failed to secure any employment and who entered the ranks of the long-term unemployed.

In this respect the experience of the recession has highlighted the inadequacy of conceptualizing the unemployed as being either a single group of people separate from the employed, or a pool of labour outside the regular labour force. For the vast majority of 'the unemployed', unemployment is a temporary state, a phase of life that will be passed through, although at the time the individual will have no way of knowing just how long that phase will last, what kind of job will be attained at the end of that phase or whether they will face further spells of unemployment. What recession does is to increase the average length of the spells of unemployment.

The structural changes we have identified above (both economic and political), have ensured that such periods of unemployment become very much a part of the experience of a large section of the working class. When we then consider that most of the new lower level service sector jobs are part-time, we find the creation of the conditions for the emergence of a large group of workers who are sub-employed, moving between spells of employment in full-time or part-time jobs and unemployment. This suggests that we may be witnessing a new division emerging between this group and those who have secured longer-term employment in the larger firms.

Another trend associated with the growth of unemployment has been the emergence of communities which have been progressively cut off from the labour market, communities to which the label 'the unemployed' meaning a group who have no experience of work, is more applicable. As we saw above, those who find it most difficult to obtain work, even in times of full employment are the unskilled, and so these workers, because of their sub-employment and low level of income even when in work, tend to be housed in low cost local authority housing. In Britain, this usually means that they are to be found concentrated in council estates. This group frequently includes many people from the various ethnic minorities who have experienced the greatest difficulty in obtaining even short-duration employment. It follows that 'the unemployed' do in fact consist of a number of different groups.

Rising levels of unemployment in these localities leads to members of these communities being the first to experience prolonged unemployment. They then become progressively cut off from the labour market, because knowledge of job vacancies, especially in areas of high unemployment, tends to flow through informal 'word of mouth' networks. If employers were to advertise vacancies they would be inundated with applications and incur the expenses of selection. By using word of mouth recruitment, these costs are avoided and the vacancy can be filled faster. However, as more and more people in a given community are made unemployed and experience difficulty in getting back into work, they become progressively excluded from the job information networks. Studies of local labour markets in some cities of the Midlands and North, have revealed communities where the majority of adults are unemployed and where young people have grown up in households in which neither parent has experienced work for a decade (Coffield, Borrill and Marshall, 1986; Ashton, Maguire and Spilsbury, 1990). National surveys such as the General Household Survey, have also shown that the unemployed tend to live in geographical concentrations more than would be expected by chance, while the DHSS cohort study found that unemployed heads of household were less likely to have working wives (Moylan, Miller and Davies, 1984). Needless to say, families in such situations may be categorized as being in poverty and face acute financial hardships which severely curtail the activities in which family members can engage.

As the few jobs that are available tend to be short-term and casual, the main source of income has to be state benefits. This generates tension and fear in the community as the consequences of being reported for breaking the rules which govern the allocation of benefits is a serious threat to the families' resources. The acute financial deprivation creates pressure for finding ways of supplementing income such as petty theft and 'fiddling', although the additional income from such 'alternative' sources is not thought to be very much.

Evidence is now accumulating that once this process of exclusion gets underway it has serious consequences for the socialization of the next generation. Young people growing up in families where the parents are unemployed perform worse at school than pupils from homes where the parents are employed (Ashton and Maguire, 1986), and there is now evidence that this may lead to the social inheritance of disadvantage as the children of the unemployed are more likely to become unemployed themselves (Payne, 1987).

During the last decade we have started to see young adults who have never experienced paid employment beginning to raise their own children (Roberts, Dench and Richardson, 1986). Once this occurs we are in the position of seeing new divisions emerge within British society, not just between those in secure jobs and those on the periphery, but more fundamentally between those with access to jobs and those who are effectively excluded from participation in the labour market. This has been referred to by some writers as an emergent 'underclass' (see Chapter 2).

A corollary of these changes has been the increasing significance of local labour markets in the determination of life chances. Given the uneven distribution of employment between the regions and the rapid decline of the traditional manufacturing industries, the ensuing distribution of employment chances has become even more skewed. Several studies on youth employment have revealed the significance of local labour markets in determining a young person's chances of experiencing unemployment and in determining the type of job they may obtain. Thus, in addition to the work of Ashton, Maguire and Spilsbury mentioned earlier, studies by Roberts, Dench and Richardson

(1986) and more recently the findings of the 16–19 Initiative (Bynner, 1990), are all showing major differences in individuals' life chances across local labour markets. For example, one study found that the children of working-class families in St Albans stood a better chance of finding middle-level, white-collar employment than did the children of middle-class families in Sunderland (Ashton, Maguire and Spilsbury, 1990).

THE PERSONAL EXPERIENCE OF UNEMPLOYMENT

For the vast majority of people who are affected by it, unemployment hurts. Some of the reasons why this should be so have been established by psychologists who have examined the functions of work against which the effects of the loss of work can be measured (Jahoda, 1982). Warr identifies nine functions of work which form the basis of mental health. For example, it provides an opportunity for the individual to exercise control; an opportunity to develop skills; it provides the individual with a variety of different experiences; it increases the availability of money and provides a valued social position. There are problems with such general theories in that not all groups experience unemployment in the same way. For some who enter unskilled work, for example, their social position may not be very highly valued but the income from it is. Thus, it may be that many of the benefits to be derived from work stem from the income it provides. After all, members of the aristocracy who did not perform paid work did not appear to suffer unduly in status terms in the past. However, what this type of approach does highlight is the need to evaluate the effects of unemployment in the context of the functions which work normally performs.

When this is done, research findings show that unemployment does damage mental health (Fryer and Payne, 1986; Banks and Ullah, 1988). Moreover, there are now enough longitudinal studies to enable us to establish that the relationship is causal, in that it is unemployment which damages the mental health rather than the person being made unemployed because they have poor mental health. In addition to mental health, studies have shown how unemployment causes a deterioration in physical health (Smith, 1987). In part this is because of the stress and anxiety it introduces as workers come to fear for their future (Cobb and Kasl, 1977).

While we can be certain that unemployment has adverse effects on mental health and general well-being, efforts to establish a deterministic sequence of stages which all the unemployed are seen to go through have been less successful. Studies of the unemployed conducted prior to the last recession on both sides of the Atlantic gave credence to the phase model of unemployment. This claimed that the unemployed moved through a series of stages in their experience of unemployment (Hayes and Nutman, 1981). After first learning of their redundant status, they experienced shock, which soon gave way to optimism that they would obtain another job. As their efforts in this sphere were unsuccessful their morale dropped until they became pessimistic about their future prospects, with their morale only rising slightly as they accepted their status as long-term unemployed.

While superficially plausible, in that it accords with the experience of many who were made redundant, there are serious flaws with this model. It was based on cross-sectional studies, with respondents being questioned about their experience of unemployment at one point in time, and results interpreted in terms of this model. There were no longitudinal studies of individuals' experience of unemployment over time, which is essential if the model is to be tested adequately. Only by following the same individuals as they moved through the various phases could we be certain of finding the evidence which would support or refute this model. As research results emerged from studies conducted during the most recent recession it became clear that not everyone reacted in the same way to the experience of unemployment (Ashton, 1986). After all, our identity is a social construct and the part that work plays in that construct is likely to differ between people in different parts of society. Thus middle-class executives who lose their jobs are likely to experience a much greater threat to their identity (Fineman, 1987) than an unskilled labourer who has already experienced a series of spells of unemployment and who knows that his or her present job was only short term. Such an unskilled worker, living in an area of high unemployment, is not likely to experience shock on becoming unemployed. The problem for him or her is likely to be acute financial deprivation which this general model underestimates. Similarly, the model ignores the experience of the minority who find unemployment a beneficial experience because it enables them to make a fresh start.

From a sociological perspective, however, it is important to locate the personal experience of the unemployed in terms of their prior location in the labour force. For it is their location within the occupational structure which largely determines the extent to which they are at risk of unemployment and the kind of resources that are available to them if and when they are made redundant (Ashton, 1986). Thus, for a middle-aged executive who has been made redundant, the redundancy may come as a shock and threaten personal identity, but the financial resources available will normally be far superior to those available to unskilled or part-time workers. Similarly for younger workers, if the person made redundant has A-levels, then he or she is far more likely to re-enter another 'good' job than if they have few qualifications and have lost a job as a skilled worker (Ashton, Maguire and Spilsbury, 1990). In a highly stratified society, where the jobs on offer provide very different prospects for the development or acquisition of skills, for the development of an identification within the occupation, for the acquisition of a highly valued status and for the financial return, it is potentially misleading to expect general models to apply uniformly throughout society.

THE WIDER CONSEQUENCES AND RAMIFICATIONS OF UNEMPLOYMENT

As we have already suggested, unemployment is unequally distributed throughout the labour force. It is those in the lower status occupations who are most at risk and what they fear is losing their income because, for them, unemployment carries with it the threat of poverty. Thus, one of the most important social consequences of high levels of unemployment is the widening of income differentials and the growth of poverty. The DHSS longitudinal study found that half of the unemployed had incomes in the bottom fifth of the earnings distribution immediately prior to unemployment (Moylan, Miller and Davies, 1984). On average the income of the household containing the unemployed person declines to around 50 – 66 per cent of what it had been previously. The work of Mack and Lansley (1985) suggests that in 1984, 58 per cent of the people living in households where the head was unemployed were poor, and nearly one-third were very poor in that they lacked a large number of the necessities of life; necessities such as having enough money to pay for public transport, a warm waterproof coat and three meals a day (Marsh, 1988). In view of the deprivation so often associated with unemployment and sub-employment it is not surprising that a number of studies have found a relationship between increases in the level of unemployment and increases in the rate of crime (Hakim, 1982).

The other consequences which the individual's experience of unemployment has on the household as a whole, is emerging from recent research. What it shows is that even when it is the male who is unemployed, it is the female who shoulders most of the emotional stress (McKee and Bell, 1986; Hartley, 1987). The personal relationships which the unemployed have tend to be more unstable and the strains are carried by all family members (Fagin and Little, 1984; Allatt and Yeadle, 1986). Once the male is unemployed the female is also likely to give up her job, in part no doubt because of the rules governing the distribution of state benefits. For those youths who cannot obtain employment this forces them to remain in a position of dependence within their family of origin. Effectively unemployment extends the period of adolescence and, as the work of Wallace (1987) has shown, leads young adults to develop new patterns of family formation.

One final problem in Britain concerns the controversy surrounding the measurement of unemployment. Just how many people are there unemployed? The official measure of unemployment is that derived from those who register for benefits, to which some of the unemployed are entitled. Because of numerous changes which have been made both to the definition of those eligible for benefits and the base figure on which the unemployment rate is calculated, it is difficult to place any great reliance on the accuracy of official figures as a measure of the 'true' rate of unemployment. The Unemployment Unit, which has provided a consistent measure based on the definition used before these changes were introduced, estimates that the official count in April 1989, which for the UK was 1 856 400 would be 2 426 200 if the original definitions were used. A more accurate definition is provided by the Labour Force Survey which asks individuals whether or not they were looking for work in the last week and the last month. This method is more reliable and picks up the married women who are looking for work but who would not be counted in the government's definition. However, it excludes those who have been discouraged from seeking work because they believe that none is available and it excludes all those who are on government schemes of one form or another. All this means that at any one point in time it is difficult to establish just how many are unemployed but we can be fairly certain that the official figures are at best only a very conservative estimate.

CONCLUSION

What we have documented in this chapter are a series of structural changes which are leading to the creation of new social divisions. These changes include the response of firms to global markets and the new labour management strategies associated with them which are introducing the division between those in the more secure jobs and those who have to eke out a living in a series of short-term, low paid jobs interspersed with periods of unemployment. This new division has also been reinforced by the destruction of many of the traditional full-time, skilled and semi-skilled jobs by the twin forces of the introduction of new technology and the effects of recession. These jobs, primarily filled by males, had provided the economic base of the old working class. In their place, the new service sector jobs have provided low skilled, part-time and often casual employment, primarily for females. This is a process which has enlarged the size of the peripheral sector as females in insecure, part-time employment join the sub-employed males with chequered career patterns. Research has also shown that those who form this peripheral sector are not evenly dispersed throughout our society, but are concentrated in limited geographical areas within some of the larger cities. These are communities which suffer high levels of long-term unemployment and are partially excluded not just from full participation in the labour market, but also from full participation in mainstream society.

There can be no doubt that the size of the peripheral sector has been increased by the political changes aimed at making the economy more competitive (Leadbeater and Lloyd, 1987). Political changes which have privatized services, reduced the legal protection afforded employees and unions and forced down wages for the lower paid, have increased the number of casual, part-time and short-term jobs and put pressure on the unemployed to accept them. As unemployment has been allowed to rise, with the cure being left to market forces, these new peripheral jobs have had to be shared by an increasing number of sub-employed people.

Not all governments have opted for this route. Others, notably those in

Sweden and Norway, have sought to contain the growth of peripheral jobs and enlarge the size of the primary sector. However, because the underlying structural changes are related to developments in the world economy, national governments cannot counteract them totally. What the experiences of these societies show is that the actions of the state can either exaggerate or contain the effects of these world-wide developments. They illustrate how the state has a degree of autonomy in its relationship with these wider economic forces. In Britain the consequences of economic and social policy have been the exacerbation of the new social divisions and the growth of the peripheral sector. Any success the government has achieved in bringing down the level of real unemployment will, of course, help reduce the size of the peripheral sector and any potential 'underclass'; but it would require new economic and social policies to diminish the emergent division between the primary and peripheral sectors.

These policy options are available at two levels. First there are the possibilities of collaborating with other members of the European Community to provide a Charter of Social Rights which would help provide a base line in terms of levels of economic security below which those who are confined to the peripheral sector would not fall. Secondly, there are a number of options at the national level which governments could follow independently of the actions of the European Community. On the one hand the state could develop an industrial and trade policy aimed at creating relatively well paid, full-time jobs and use its powers as an employer to enhance the quality of existing jobs. It could also use its welfare and legislative powers to minimize the impact of the economic and social consequences of the new divisions.

An effective industrial and trade policy would be necessary to encourage a manufacturing sector which was able to compete more effectively in the type of highly developed product markets where companies are still creating well paid, full-time jobs. This would mean abandoning the policy of leaving the direction of the economy to 'market forces' and instead using the combined resources of industry, labour organizations and the state to target those parts of the international product markets where it is believed that British based firms could compete effectively. Similar policies have been adopted by the Swedish and Japanese governments. It would also mean using the government's power as an employer to improve the quality in terms of both levels of pay and job security in the public sector and reduce the progressive reliance on the exploitation of subcontract labour. Such policies would both enhance the rate at which 'good quality' jobs were created and reduce the rate at which the new peripheral sector jobs are growing. However, this would not eliminate the emergence of peripheral sector jobs, because such jobs are a product of the changes in the global division of labour and in the concentration of capital in the service sector, which, in many respects, are forces outside the direct control of the state in capitalist societies.

To counteract the divisive impact of these broader structural changes, the state does have a range of welfare the legislative powers it could use. For example, an active labour market policy such as that followed in Sweden could help reduce unemployment and retrain labour for employment in the newer industries. Employment protection legislation can help reduce the insecurities of the labour market. However, even these measures would still leave us with the problem of how to motivate people to take the low paid part-time jobs which are still regarded as essential by employers. Here the strategy would be to abandon existing attempts to cut back on welfare payments in an effort to force people to accept such jobs and instead institute a policy of providing a universal minimum income which would then be supplemented by income from paid employment, either full-time or part-time. Once again we would stress that these policies would not eradicate these emergent social divisions but they would function to minimize their impact on the life chances of those affected by them.

4
Emerging 'alternatives' to full-time and permanent employment*

RALPH FEVRE

INTRODUCTION

Over the last 20 or 30 years, people living in industrialized countries have come to think of paid work in terms of a rather simplified stereotype. The closest approximation to this stereotype might be car-assembly work such as that described by Huw Beynon in *Working for Ford* (1973). The workers who did this sort of work were *men* who had received limited job training and were not called upon to do work which fell outside that job. They were usually members of trade unions, and it was through national negotiations between unions and employers (with some assistance from the state) that they were guaranteed standard wages, standard hours of work, standard contracts of employment and job security (or compensation for insecurity). Such workers could expect to work on a limited range of tasks which made up a particular job or occupation, and to do this for 40 hours a week, for 48 weeks a year, until they retired. If they left work, they quit voluntarily or, much more rarely, were dismissed. They were hardly ever made redundant.

This somewhat naive stereotype always ignored the fact that large sections of the manual working class were rather less fortunate and remained vulnerable; for example, to spells of short-time work and even unemployment. In recent years every aspect of this stereotype of work in industrialized countries has been challenged by sociologists and other social scientists. For example, it is now frequently pointed out that *women* may make up at least 50 per cent of the paid workforce in such countries. In this chapter, however, we will only examine challenges to particular aspects of the stereotype, namely its assumption that typical work involves *full-time, permanent employment*.

'Non-standard' (paid) work is understood as the opposite of this type: work which is either part-time, temporary, or (as in self-employment) does not involve a conventional contract of employment. There is certainly a great deal of evidence to suggest that non-standard work is what a lot of people do. The preliminary results of the 1988 Labour Force Survey[1] indicated that 1 385 000 people in Great Britain were in temporary work while a further 519 000 people were working on (temporary) government employment and training schemes. Over five million (5 406 000) were in part-time work, and 3 155 000 were self-employed. In summary, 5.6 per cent of all the employed and self-employed were temporary, 22 per cent were part-time and 13 per cent were self-employed.

There is small virtue in simply correcting a stereotype. In this chapter we will try to find answers to more difficult questions. Firstly, is there a *trend* towards non-standard jobs in Britain? The proportion of full-time, permanent employees has declined, especially in manufacturing industry, because of falling demand for companies' products and/or increased productivity (particularly following technological change). But is there any evidence of an absolute (rather than relative) increase in non-standard jobs? If there is, has this increase been caused by employers who have switched from full-time, permanent employment to non-standard forms of work or has growth occurred for some other reason? Secondly, what might *employers* gain from a move to non-standard work? Furthermore, what does non-standard work mean for the people who do it? Is it 'poor work', and are non-standard jobs necessarily 'sub-standard' jobs? Finally, does the pattern of non-standard work in the late 1980s contain any hints of future trends in forms of work?

IS NON-STANDARD WORK INCREASING?

Statistical evidence of a *general* trend towards non-standard work is scarce and unreliable. To a large extent, researchers have been forced to rely on a single series of figures – the official Labour Force Survey – but this series has not always proved reliable. For example, in the mid-1980s some researchers were misled by an error in official statistics (see below). Other researchers have pointed out that the definitions used to count non-standard jobs are confusing and ambiguous. Furthermore, these definitions have been changed during the 1980s and so year-to-year comparisons can be difficult or impossible.

Even when researchers have felt able to trust the official statistics, they have frequently found that the trends which the figures measure are confused. Statistics for the second-half of the 1980s suggest that while a change may have occurred at the time of the 'shake-out' at the beginning of the decade, this did not become a more general trend, and there are even signs of a later reversal of the trend. The most recent figures (1984–1988) are reproduced in some detail below because they may well give the best guide as to the likely trends in the 1990s.

Pollert (1987, 1988a, b) and Casey (1987) have done most to deflate original claims of a revolutionary switch to non-standard work in Britain.

Early estimates of increases in temporary working were influenced by errors in official figures and both writers consider that there has been little growth in temporary employment, except in respect of employment on government schemes. Employers' use of temporary workers – especially of *casual* workers (Fevre, 1989) – increased in the early 1980s but comparison with more recent Labour Force Surveys up to 1988 confirms that the growth of temporary work has, at best, been slow and hesitant. The number of men who were temporary workers grew by 7 per cent between 1984 and 1988, while the number of women temporaries grew by 5 per cent. The temporary proportion of all employees and the self-employed remains small (4.3 per cent for men and 7.4 per cent for women). However the Labour Force Survey also provides information on the experience of temporary work amongst the unemployed.

The 1987 Survey[2] showed that 376 000 unemployed people in Great Britain had become unemployed because their last job was a temporary one which had come to an end. This means that nearly one in eight of the unemployed were ex-temporary workers; a statistic that shows temporary work is rather more important to some workers than aggregate figures might suggest.

There has been genuine growth in part-time working and self-employment. The Labour Force Survey shows that the number of part-time employees increased by 17 per cent for women (who made up 88 per cent of part-time workers in 1988), and 61 per cent for men, between 1981 and 1988. The numbers of self-employed also increased throughout the 1980s. Between 1984 and 1988, for example, the numbers of full-time, self-employed men grew by 20 per cent, while the number of women in this category grew by 30 per cent.

The Labour Force Survey figures for part-timers and the self-employed (and temporaries) are inflated by double counting since the same people can appear in more than one category in the survey. Thus, in 1988, 516 000 people who were both self-employed and part-time were counted twice. However, this double counting is matched by a large amount of 'hidden' part-time, self-employed (and possibly temporary) work. By 1988 nearly one million people in Great Britain had second jobs. If we assume that all of these second jobs were part-time[3] we can add an extra 967 000 to the part-time total. On the other hand, nearly one-third of all second jobs (compared to one in eight of all jobs) involve self-employment, so we might choose to add an extra 310 000 to the numbers of self-employed. The number of second jobs of all types has been increasing but there was an especially sharp increase between 1987 and 1988, particularly for men.

What sort of workers take non-standard jobs? For the most part, they are women. Married women have always been over-represented in part-time work and under-represented in full-time, permanent employment. Indeed, the net gain in employment in Britain in the 1980s can largely be explained by reference to the growth of part-time jobs taken by women. Nevertheless, the gender bias in various types of non-standard work is perhaps less obvious than it has been in the recent past.

In the late 1980s temporary work remained fairly equally divided between men and women. Women were, of course, in the great majority in part-time work, but the rate of growth in part-time employment between 1981 and 1988 was far higher for men that that for women. In respect of (part-time) *second* jobs, the rate of growth for women increased up to 1987 but in the following year there was 'an unprecedented increase in the number of men with a second job' (*Employment Gazette*, April 1989). Older workers retain a large share of part-time jobs: according to the 1987 Labour Force Survey, 9 per cent of male employees or self-employed aged 60–64 were part-time, whereas 76 per cent of married women between 60 and 64 were part-time workers. Younger workers are also more likely to work part-time. The 1987 Labour Force Survey showed that 9 per cent of 16–19-year olds with jobs worked part-time. The 1988 Survey confirmed a sharp increase in the numbers of people who were doing part-time work because they were students or still at school. One-third of men and nearly one-third of non-married women (non-married women part-timers outnumber all men part-timers) who worked part-time said this was their reason for not doing full-time work.

Self-employment has increased in general, but the fastest rate of growth has been among women. For example, there was a 30 per cent increase in the number of full-time, self-employed women between 1984 and 1988. Once second jobs are taken into account, the share of self-employment held by women has increased and so has the rate at which women are increasing their share.

In summary, married women may still make up the majority of part-time workers but there is an increasing number of men (and non-married women), especially those aged under 19 or over 60, who work part-time. In self-employment (where *men* have traditionally been in the majority), the trend is reversed. Most of the self-employed (although not the part-time self-employed) are men, but the fastest rate of growth in self-employment is found amongst women.

When we come to consider non-standard work from the employers' viewpoint, we may want to distinguish between different *types* of employers. It is therefore necessary to ask, at this stage, which employers have increased their use of non-standard forms of work. Although the broader picture is sometimes confused, Pollert (1987, 1988a, b) is adamant that any revolution in forms of work that has taken place has not occurred in British manufacturing industry. The number of temporaries in manufacturing has actually fallen, and any significant increases in non-standard (especially part-time) work in private industry has occurred in those industries which have always had it, namely the *service* industries like hotels and catering.

The 1987 Census of Employment (Employment Gazette, October 1989) showed that the vast majority of part-time employees in the UK worked in service industries. Part-timers made up 12 per cent of male and 47 per cent of female employees in services compared to less than 1 per cent of male and 17 per cent of female employees in a manufacturing sector like metal goods, engineering and vehicles. Even those manufacturing industries – bread, flour and confectionery; clothing; newspaper printing – with significant numbers of part-timers, generally had much lower proportions of part-timers than the service industries as a whole. Within the service sector, retail distribution, hotels and catering, 'other services' and education all had more part-time women workers than full-time women workers. In hotels and catering, part-timers constituted 58 per cent of *all* employees.

These patterns were repeated for the self-employed. Although self-employment in production increased by 76 per cent between 1981 and 1988, the rate of increase in service industries (which provide work for most of the self-employed) was similar or even greater. The 1988 Labour Force Survey showed that nearly a quarter of self-employed women were in retail distribution, 12.5 per cent were in hotels and catering, and over 33 per cent worked in 'other services'. Roughly 50 per cent of the male self-employed worked in retail distribution or banking, finance and business services; and over 25 per cent worked in the construction industry (see note 4 below).

Given that non-standard forms of work have always been important to service sector employers, the 'revolutionary' change in the private sector turns out to be a rediscovery of something previously neglected. Any overall increase in the number or proportion of non-standard jobs in the private sector can be explained (also see MacInnes, 1987), for the most part, by the overall expansion of service sector jobs which began in Britain in the 1970s (and by reductions in the total number of workers of all types in manufacturing where such jobs are less common).[4]

The *occupational* distribution of non-standard jobs is also relevant to the discussion of employers, and to the discussion of the nature of non-standard jobs which follows. Unfortunately the Labour Force Survey does not provide a very detailed analysis of occupations. Nevertheless, Dale and Bamford (1988) were able to conclude from the survey that the occupational distribution of temporary workers differed from that of permanent workers. Casual temporaries were over-represented in selling and clerical occupations and in personal services (for example, school helpers, cleaners, waitresses and bar-tenders). Temporaries working on a fixed-term contract were over-represented in health, education and welfare occupations and in skilled and unskilled jobs amongst metal and electric, and construction occupations.

It is probable that the most important recent change which is reflected in these patterns is the increase in non-standard forms of work amongst non-manual workers, including professionals and managers (also see Hogarth and Daniel, 1988, p. 38). Dale and Bamford observe that 25 per cent of all temporaries on contracts are classified in professional occupations and in health, education and welfare occupations. Most of these workers are in fact employed in the public sector: 'nurses, medical practitioners and teachers in both schools and higher education are particularly prevalent' (Dale and Bamford, 1989, p. 201).

These observations suggest that any revolutionary shift to non-standard forms of work has not occurred in private sector manufacturing, or even services, but in the *public* sector (including those parts of the public sector which have subsequently experienced some form of privatization). According to Pollert, the most significant increase in temporary and part-time working has taken place in public sector services. This finding has been confirmed – for all categories of non-standard work – in both public sector services and in other types of public sector employment, including manufacturing (Ascher, 1987; Fevre, 1989). The public sector appears to have made the changes which were once predicted for private manufacturing.

IS NON-STANDARD WORK GOOD FOR EMPLOYERS?

Twenty years ago, a few researchers in the USA began to write about systematic variations in the types of jobs which were offered by employers. Doeringer and Piore (1971) proved to be the most influential of these writers. They concluded that jobs of the type we have described as 'non-standard' were usually offered by 'secondary' *less successful* employers. 'Primary' employers were far more likely to use the stereotyped form of employment described at the beginning of this chapter. Other writers, for example Friedman (1978) pointed out that the same employer might have a use for both forms, but it was not until the mid-1980s that the majority of researchers began to wonder whether many employers, perhaps all employers, might benefit if they switched to non-standard forms of work. The key to this change in thinking was the revelation (to some) that non-standard jobs offered *flexibility* to employers.

Increased attention to 'flexible' work produced a 'flexibility debate' in the social science literature (see, for example Pollert, forthcoming). This debate concerned the facts of the case (was flexible work increasing and, if so, why?) and the implications (if any) for theory. Writers who engaged in either or both of these aspects of the debate frequently took the work of John Atkinson (1984a, b) on the 'flexible firm' as their starting point. Atkinson produced a model of organization which suggested firms were, or should be, moving towards a new set of arrangements with those who supplied them with labour. A small core of full-time, permanent employees would be complemented by a variety of 'flexible workers' who would be paid only when their labour was actually required.

At this point, readers should note that the sort of 'flexibility' described by Atkinson should not be confused with work on 'flexible specialization' inspired by Piore and Sabel (1984). Although Piore and Sabel's research was often discussed in the same books, papers and conferences which dealt with

Atkinson's work, Piore and Sabel were not concerned with non-standard jobs. While they challenged some aspects of the stereotype of paid employment described at the beginning of this chapter, they were really concerned with changes in the tasks which people did when they were at work, and particularly with signs of a shift away from narrow occupational specialization to a work-force which was 'flexible' in the sense that it could be used in a variety of different ways. Individual workers might, for example, offer employers a variety of different occupational skills (electrician, welder, fitter) rather than one alone. Piore and Sabel's work has received extensive criticism (see, for example, Williams *et al.*, 1987), but the merits of their case are not under discussion here. All that matters is that 'functional flexibility' in Piore and Sabel's sense of variation in the type of labour that workers perform during the hours they are at work should not be confused with 'flexibility' arising from non-standard forms of work.

The flexible advantages of non-standard forms of work have been conceived in a variety of ways (Meulders and Wilkin, 1987), but the most important benefits would appear to fall into two categories: 'numerical flexibility' and 'wage flexibility'.

Numerical flexibility

Non-standard jobs allow those who *pay* for labour to match their payments more closely to the work done. The employer of full-time, permanent employees is frequently (Bowers, Deaton and Turk, 1982) faced with a choice between carrying more labour than s/he needs (at times when less work is needed) and paying overtime rates (when more work is needed). Flexible workers offer a third alternative since they are only paid when their work is required. Flexible work gives those who pay for labour an advantage in that they only have to use (and pay for) the volume of ingredients required by the recipe and need not have half-empty packets on the shelf or find themselves short of a couple of eggs for the pudding. It is easy enough to see how temporary workers provide employers with flexibility. Temporaries (especially casuals) need only be paid when there is work for them to do. But what of the other types of non-standard jobs – part-time jobs (by far the most common) and self-employment?

There is some disagreement (Michon, 1987; Pollert, 1988a) as to whether part-time work is flexible at all, but it would appear to offer similar advantages to employers. Temporaries are only paid for the days, weeks or months when their labour is fully utilized and part-timers are only paid for the hours when their labour is fully utilized. The same principle applies in each case: either form of non-standard work allows employers to avoid paying wages when workers are not needed. In addition, employers may find that it is easier and cheaper to persuade part-timers to vary their hours (or easier and cheaper to sack part-timers) when their demand for labour varies.

Objections to the description of the self-employed as flexible workers take a different form. Here the important point to grasp is that many self-employed workers are in effect temporaries engaged by employers on a different legal basis:

> A significant proportion of so called self employed people are no more than employees by another name. They just lack the security of a contract of employment, and are responsible for their own National Insurance contributions . . . many are extremely low paid. (*Unemployment Bulletin*, Summer 1989; see also Casey and Creigh, 1988; Hakim, 1988)

In fact, much of the literature on numerical flexibility refers not simply to the self-employed but to firms which work on contract or subcontract to other firms. Contractors and subcontractors (hereafter, 'sub/contractors') are believed to offer much the same advantages to employers as non-standard forms of work: managers can contract other firms in place of full-time, permanent employees – in order to reduce unnecessary costs and make their firm more responsive to changes in demand – in exactly the same way as they might use temporary workers.

It is not for this reason, however, that reference is made to sub/contractors in this chapter. Rather, they deserve a mention simply because non-standard forms of work of all types are especially prevalent within sub/contractors. This would seem to indicate that any expansion of sub/contracting might help to explain the growth in non-standard jobs, but readers should note that there is no clear evidence of a general increase in sub/contracting (Pollert, 1988a, b). On the other hand, official figures are even more unreliable in respect of sub/contracting (Fevre, 1989, p. 155n) than in the case of non-standard work. The use of sub/contractors has certainly increased in some sectors (see, for example, Marginson *et al.*, 1988), especially in those sectors where the number of non-standard jobs has grown, for example in public sector services (Ascher, 1987) and public sector manufacturing (Fevre, 1989).

Wage flexibility

In the 1980s, some researchers also pointed out that, for various reasons (for example, a change in the relative bargaining power of workers and managers), it might be that those who used flexible workers did not simply use the right volume of ingredients in their recipes (not too much and not too little) but paid less than others for the ingredients (the labour they needed) in the first place.

The problem of 'wage flexibility' has preoccupied British economists for some time. Economists usually assume that increased unemployment will reduce the wages of those in work, and some economists confessed themselves baffled when British wages did not fall with rising unemployment after 1979. For example, Leadbeater and Lloyd (1987):

> Mrs Thatcher's former economic adviser, Professor Alan Walters, also admits that the obstinacy of wage setting in the face of high unemployment is a 'mystery'. (p. 51)

There are several good reasons why wages have not adjusted and a useful summary of explanations for 'obstinate wage-setting' is given by Batstone and Gourlay (1986). They explain why the 'simple price auction model' – in which an unemployed worker offers to work for lower wages – is flawed in this way:

> Even in a non-union situation, employers are unlikely to conform to the price-auction model, simply because of the very large transaction costs involved. These would relate to a massive and unpredictable flow of applicants who would have to be assessed; there would be the costs involved in sacking more highly paid workers; there would be continual disruptions to production as replacement labour was introduced and as new workers had to learn their tasks (if only in terms of tacit skills). The administration of steadily declining wage rates would be a major task; team working would be continually disrupted and so on. In short, this pattern of continual, atomistic bargaining would lead to a total shambles . . . (p. 6)

Batstone and Gourlay then add several 'more important' reasons to explain the failure of the price-auction model: 'internal labour markets' and associated non-wage factors which buy workers' co-operation in efficient working and the resistance of unions to 'atomistic bargaining'. It appears, however, that employers have found a way round some of these problems. Samuel Brittan writes:

> The British insistence on the 'rate for the job' makes a two-tier wages system difficult to establish formally. But the trend towards cheaper contract labour is an informal move in that direction. (Leadbeater and Lloyd, 1987, p. 68)

In a 'two-tier wages system' workers accept that those who are recruited from the ranks of the unemployed will receive lower wages than those currently in employment. In the USA, particularly in non-union firms, workers have been formally obliged to recognize this differential in the form of two-tier wage systems for permanent, full-time employees; but in the UK such systems are usually less formal and almost always comprise two or more different categories of worker. The top, higher paid tier is made up of permanent, full-time staff who belong to trade unions; the lower tier is occupied by temporaries, part-timers, the self-employed and the employees of sub/contractors[5] who do not belong to trade unions or who are neglected by their trade unions. In other words, some British employers have been able to bring wages down (to reflect rising unemployment) by keeping in place, or even enhancing, existing arrangements for their current employees (or for those employees who remain if redundancies occur) and by hiring new labour in the form of flexible workers. They have even sacked full-time, permanent employees and re-hired them in non-standard jobs.

Any two-tier system will help to solve the practical problems of making labour cheaper (the necessity for team working, tacit skills, and so on) because the bottom tier is not continually renewed (as it would be in 'atomistic wage bargaining'). The (informal) British version of the two-tier system also solves these problems too: part-timers, for example, remain a part of the workforce. Individual temporaries, self-employed and workers with sub/contractors will move in and out of the workforce but the company recruits from a pool of labour which soon acquires experience, tacit skills and so on. The pool may even consist of workers who were once employed as permanent, full-time employees of the company who were recently made redundant (Fevre, 1989). The informal solution also solves implementation problems (including, but not only, the resistance of existing workers and their trade unions). For example, existing employees do not object because the company is not reducing wages in their category – full-time, permanent, employee – of labour. Trade unions do not object because they are not concerned with negotiating the wages and conditions of the second tier, and/or because established (wage) differentials (with flexible workers) will remain or may even increase.

It is rarely noted that the informal version of the two-tier system is potentially more attractive (to employers) than the formal version because it ensures that the two-tier system will not deteriorate once it is in place. In the informal version, flexible workers will continue to be disciplined by the expectation of future unemployment even while they are (temporarily) in work (Fevre, 1989). Those at the bottom of a formal two-tier system may lose the memory of their unhappy experience in the labour market after a while and begin to press for the same treatment as those in the upper tier. This will not happen in the case of temporaries and the self-employed because their labour market experience will continue.

Furthermore, workers at the bottom of a formal two-tier system are hired at a standard (albeit lower) rate of wages. If they demand higher wages they may well do so collectively. An employer who resists this pressure will be forced to sack the lot and re-hire another group of workers. Employers who use an informal system are much less likely to come up against such problems (and have established practices for hiring large numbers of workers even if they do). The wages of workers in their bottom tier may well vary from one individual to another, and it is probable that demands for improved wages will come from individuals or small groups. Such demands can more easily be met with the sack because the employer is not put to the expense of hiring a new bottom tier in order to keep wages low. S/he simply has to do a little more fishing in the pool of flexible workers than usual. In summary, the informal version of wage flexibility produces something very close to 'atomistic wage bargaining' but without many of the disadvantages of such a system of pay determination.

IS NON-STANDARD WORK GOOD FOR WORKERS?

We can conclude from the preceding section that where employers see non-standard work as 'flexible' work, then the workers who do it may well regard it as 'poor work'. 'Numerical flexibility' suggests that workers have less time at work, that is, less opportunity to earn incomes. 'Wage flexibility' suggests that they earn less income even when they have such opportunities.

There is certainly evidence to show that non-standard jobs have, in general, always been less attractive (Pollert, 1988a), and that they have remained less attractive than full-time, permanent jobs in the 1980s (see, for example *Low Pay Review*, Spring and Autumn 1987; *Guardian*, 20 December 1989). Where employers reduce their wage bills by way of 'numerical flexibility', this must reduce workers' incomes unless they can gain enough work from different employers to give them an income comparable to that of full-time, permanent employees. This disadvantage (to workers) is rarely compensated by improvements in wage rates (or other rewards) or by easier or more pleasant work. Indeed, 'wage flexibility' means that workers in non-standard jobs receive lower hourly wages than other workers do, but work harder.

The 1987 Census of Employment shows that part-timers, for example, are consistently over-represented in low paying industries, and even within individual industries part-timers receive lower hourly earnings than full-time workers (see, for example, *Employment Gazette*, April 1989). Inland Revenue statistics show that 45 per cent of self-employed people had a gross income from self-employment of less than £5 000 in 1985–1986 (*Unemployment Bulletin*, Summer 1989). Thus most workers in non-standard jobs get *less* rewards (lower pay, no pension or sick pay) in return for *greater* inconvenience (harder work and poor working conditions).

Non-standard jobs also have other disadvantages which only become clear in the longer term. First, the *insecurity* of many of these jobs means that workers are unable to predict their income in the same way as full-time, permanent employees (Potter, 1987; Pollert, 1988a, b). It is no longer a case of loosing your livelihood because of the rare chance of dismissal, or even loosing it (with compensation) through early retirement or mass redundancy. Even in the case of part-timers, employers will generally find it easier and less costly to dispense with their labour. Furthermore, workers are less able to improve their income when in work because the further effects of 'wage flexibility' lead to their exclusion from pay scales, career structures and training programmes.

There is also evidence (Coyle, 1987; Fevre, 1987, 1989; *Listener*, 12

November 1987; Evans and Lewis, forthcoming) that, on many counts, non-standard work is now even less attractive than it has been in the recent past[6]: proportionately more non-standard work is now found in the least attractive sorts of non-standard jobs and non-standard work in general has deteriorated. For example, the supply of temporary work has become less predictable while spells of temporary work have become shorter and more likely to alternate with spells of unemployment. Proportionately fewer temporary workers are in a position to put together a 'portfolio' of temporary jobs which provides an income commensurate with full-time permanent employment (Harris *et al.*, 1987; Ford, 1989) and it should be noted that this is not the case amongst most part-timers or the self-employed.

Similarly, as the number of non-standard jobs increases, the proportion of workers which receive some compensation in the shape of higher wages or other benefits – for the inherent disadvantages of lower, unpredictable incomes – has fallen. Some non-standard jobs are still more attractive than others but there has been a general deterioration. Thus those in the worst sorts of work have found that there has been an absolute deterioration in what were already very unattractive jobs. For example, those in the lowest paid casual work (perhaps off-the-books) find that it is harder, more unhealthy and more dangerous than before.

Furthermore, new evidence is emerging (Mackay, forthcoming) which suggests that flexible workers suffer a double disadvantage; not only are they less likely to be in work, and receive less income from this work, but they may well receive less income (in the form of welfare benefits) when they are *out of work*. Flexible workers, like others who have experienced unemployment in Britain in the 1980s, have suffered when welfare benefits have not been increased in line with inflation. But new evidence supports something only hinted at in earlier small-scale research: flexible workers are also to be found amongst the growing number of workers who are disqualified from receiving benefits altogether (and are therefore excluded from official unemployment figures).

Finally, it should be mentioned that non-standard forms of work have been extended to cover groups of workers who have not experienced it before. Most of these workers would have good reason to be less satisfied with non-standard work than with their previous jobs. For example, the married women part-timers who made up the bulk of the new non-standard workforce in the 1980s had, for the most part, been accustomed to full-time, permanent employment before they re-entered the labour force (in non-standard jobs) after having children. Public sector workers – for example, those in the National Health Service (and in the British Steel Corporation before privatization) – are often more or less directly transferred from full-time, permanent employment to non-standard jobs. Although many older men become long-term unemployed (or leave the labour market altogether) after losing full-time, permanent jobs, some are forced into non-standard work in the absence of other jobs. In addition, many young workers who entered the labour market for the first time in the 1980s would have expected full-time, permanent jobs if they had been starting work a few years earlier. Instead, new workers, for example professionals and managers and a variety of workers in education (Millward and Stevens, 1986; Leighton, 1987), find themselves in non-standard jobs.

Despite all the evidence presented above, it would nevertheless be foolish to conclude that all workers doing non-standard jobs would rather be full-time, permanent employees. According to the Labour Force Survey,[7] the majority of temporary workers are not doing temporary work because they cannot find permanent jobs, and the proportion in the 'conscript' category is falling. It can be argued, therefore, that temporaries choose this kind of work because it brings autonomy and variety. Similarly, it might be pointed out that by far the most important group of part-time workers are married women. Married women, whether or not they have children under school age, are assumed to prefer part-time work because they do not want to work full-time. Finally, the self-employed are often assumed to be budding artisans or entrepreneurs who are only waiting for redundancy (and redundancy pay) or an enterprise allowance in order to fulfil their desire for the rewards (financial and otherwise) of self-employment.

Yet, while it is clear that workers who are conscripted into temporary or part-time work are not getting the working arrangements they would prefer, it is also true that even those who want temporary or part-time work are actually paying their employers a *premium* for the privilege. The existence of this premium has already been noted in the discussion of 'wage flexibility': if 'flexible' workers were not receiving lower wages (and fewer fringe benefits and working harder) then there would be no wage flexibility at all! If workers try to recoup the premium they pay to employers, by doing two jobs for example, then they lose whatever benefits they sought from non-standard working arrangements in the first place. In these circumstances it makes little sense to say that those workers who want non-standard arrangements have 'chosen' current patterns of non-standard work. Similarly, employers limit workers' freedom of choice by their omissions as much as by their commissions: those few employers who provide creches, for example, give working parents a *real* choice of working arrangements.

NON-STANDARD WORK IN THE 1990S

There are two reasons to believe that non-standard forms of work will continue to increase in the 1990s. In the first place, the growth of non-standard jobs in the 1980s accompanied the expansion of employment in the privately-owned service sector and a switch to non-standard work in the public sector. It is likely that both of these trends will continue, although at a slower pace. Secondly, the growth of non-standard jobs in the 1980s took place at a time when more workers wanted non-standard jobs or, at the least, were prepared to take them. This trend is also likely to continue since the proportion of the labour force which will take non-standard jobs is scheduled to rise.

We can conclude that a slow but steady growth in non-standard jobs will (probably) continue in the 1990s, but will these non-standard jobs be any better than those created in the previous decade? In the 1980s more and more employers and workers wanted non-standard jobs, but the workers rarely got the sort of non-standard work they would have preferred. At present, those who want full-time, permanent employment become unemployed or are conscripted as flexible workers. Those who want non-standard jobs may also be unemployed (although perhaps not counted as such), or pay a premium for the satisfaction of this wish, or end up with two jobs and rather more hours of work (for less rewards) than full-time, permanent employees. Will this also be the pattern in the immediate future?

Perhaps few workers would mind if the stereotyped employment pattern described at the beginning of this chapter was banished to the pages of history. Few would regret the passing of the eight-to-five job which entailed a life sentence of monotony at work and the domination of workers' lives outside work by the rigid patterns imposed by their contracts of employment. More and more workers are demanding increased flexibility from their work (see, for example, Hogarth and Daniel, 1988; Dey, 1989; *Independent*, 25 October 1989; *Guardian*, 20 December 1989). They want flexible time-keeping, career breaks and parental leave, that is, they want flexible employers. A more flexible attitude from employers in respect of these and other innovations, such as employers' provision of child-care facilities and greater enthusiasm to relocate to areas with abundant labour, might solve a variety of problems ranging from traffic congestion and high property prices in the south east of England to the waste of human resources implied by the current employment patterns of married women with children and regional unemployment.

The general principle of employer flexibility is in fact easy to grasp: increasing numbers of workers feel that other things (their partners, children, leisure time, 'quality of life') are just as important as paid work. If they are to be continually asked to choose between the two then they cannot enjoy work or give of their best as workers. This principle is clearly a far cry from the existing patterns of worker flexibility described here, as one of the originators of the 'flexibility' literature acknowledges (Atkinson, 1987). What are the prospects of future convergence? Can we expect that, in the near future the types of non-standard work offered by employers will offer the workforce the flexibility they increasingly want from their work?

Atkinson (1987) considers the possibilities of improvements in non-standard work arising from the activity of trade unions and from government legislation. But change of this type would appear to depend on other changes – for example, changes in government policies or Britain's adoption of the full European Social Charter – which cannot be predicted with certainty. Similarly, we are unable to say with any degree of confidence whether continued economic growth in the 1990s will lead to lower unemployment and tighter labour markets which might shift the balance of bargaining power from employers to workers, and so lead to improvements in non-standard jobs.

There is, however, one trend that can be predicted with confidence. British employers will shortly be faced with a shortage of young workers. Will this lead to an improvement in non-standard jobs; in particular, will employers find workers to replace the missing school-leavers amongst those who want (good) non-standard jobs? For example, will employers be forced to increase the rewards of part-time work so that they can recruit married women in order to make up for the reduced supply of younger workers?

It may be too early to tell, but there are few signs that employers are improving non-standard jobs in response to the 'demographic time bomb', despite frequent exhortations (sometimes from the government) to do so (see, for example, *Independent*, 25 October 1989). On the existing evidence, we must conclude that, so long as those employers who use non-standard forms of work regard labour as a cost which must be reduced, rather than as a resource which should be valued (MacInnes, 1987; see Fevre, forthcoming), there is a danger that employers will neglect to improve non-standard jobs. Instead, the 1990s may bring high labour turnover and labour shortages to such employers while the prospect of good non-standard jobs remains tantalizingly out of the reach of most workers.

NOTES

* I wish to acknowledge the useful comments and suggestions I have received while preparing this chapter from David Jones, Ross Mackay and the editors of this volume.

1 Labour Force Survey data and interpretation cited in this chapter can be found in *Employment Gazette*, April 1989; Office of Population Censuses and Surveys (1987, 1989); and *Unemployment Bulletin*, Summer, 1989.

2 The full 1988 Labour Force Survey results were not released at the time of writing.

3 Indeed the majority of second jobs were held by people who worked full-time in their 'main' jobs.

4 Employers in the UK *construction* industry have also traditionally made use of non-standard forms of work; however, there is evidence to suggest that the industry has increased this use still further in recent times (Evans and Lewis, forthcoming). Nevertheless, this trend began in the 1970s and the construction industry example offers no more support for the notion of a revolutionary change than does the service sector.

5 In some cases employers are only able to install a two-tier system by enlisting the help of sub/contractors and so formally segregating the second tier from the full-time, permanent workforce.

6 This often happens where the growth in flexible working has taken place in *new* firms (Fevre, 1987).

7 Readers should note the high (and rising) totals for 'other reasons' given in the Labour Force Survey by those who do part-time or temporary work.

5

Women's poor work

LYDIA MORRIS

INTRODUCTION

One topic which has been the focus of both heightened public concern and growing sociological interest is the increased presence of women, and particularly married women in the labour force. In 1881 women constituted 27 per cent of the UK labour force, a figure which had risen to 33.6 per cent by 1948 and 43 per cent by 1984 (see Dex, 1985 and *Employment Gazette*, January 1987). These changes translate into a gradual rise in the proportion of the female work-force made up of *married* women; from 38 per cent in 1951 to 63 and 64 per cent in 1971 and 1985 respectively (see General Household Survey, 1985, Table 6.24). The sociological challenge posed by this change has spawned a number of different approaches to women's employment, from household divisions of labour (Pahl, 1984) to labour market segregation (Walby, 1989) and the significance of the woman's wage (Morris with Ruane, 1989). But equally interesting is the sociological significance of the nature of popular interest in married women's employment.

Firstly there is the implicit assumption that married women's employment is in some sense remarkable because these women have available some other source of support, namely husbands. Secondly and in contrast, there is an assumption that gender roles have been fundamentally challenged by the increasing employment of married women, especially at a time of high male unemployment. Both these reactions to married women's employment are illuminated by a discussion of the employment options open to married women, and a more general understanding of married women's position in the labour market. The low level of women's pay itself seems to presuppose some additional source of support and would in fact be inadequate as a principal household wage, whilst research has shown (for example, Morris,

1987, 1988) that in failing to equal benefit levels women's earnings do not, in the majority of cases, prompt a 'role reversal' response to male unemployment. These issues are in a sense related to women's traditional position in the domestic sphere.

The intention in this chapter is to highlight and explore the nature of this relationship. The chapter begins with a brief summary of the theoretical approaches to women's employment, noting the explanatory flaws in a number of the available perspectives. The issues most neglected concern women's terms of entry into paid employment, the relationship between women's labour market and household positions, the dynamics of household finance, access to and adequacy of the male wage, and the structuring of employment opportunities for women.

Whilst these issues will be shown often to be interrelated it should be noted at the outset that there is considerable variety in women's employment patterns according, for example, to class position, marital status, ethnic identity, and so on. The focus of this chapter is on women's disadvantaged employment position, and why it is that certain sections of the female population have come to be concentrated in particular types of employment. The discussion to follow is not therefore intended to cover all aspects of women's employment, but rather to examine certain aspects of their 'poor work' and the adequacy of the theoretical perspectives which have been used in attempts at explanation.

DUAL ROLES AND DUAL MARKETS

An implicit acceptance of women's domestic role underlay work in the fifties which approached married women's employment from the perspective of their dual roles. Here the concentration, as in Myrdal and Klein's work (1956), is on the tension deriving from the two roles of housewife and worker (see Beechey, 1987 for review). Given that such accounts start from an acceptance of traditional gender roles they do not raise explanatory issues, or indeed aspire to do so. They have, however, led to assessments of 'role strain' (see Pleck, 1985 for review), calculations of relative benefits set against inherent stress, and over-optimistic accounts of the marriage of the future.

Predictions that women's employment will produce an equalization of men's and women's roles inside and outside the home (for example, Blood and Wolfe, 1960) have now been firmly discredited (see Morris, 1988 for review). Quite apart from men's failure to assume a fair share of the domestic burden any 'optimistic' view of the potential for change in gender roles neglects to consider the fact that men and women, and especially married women, are differentially located in the labour market. Acknowledgement of this fact prompts two additional steps to be taken; an examination of the organization of production and a questioning of why women enter the labour market on different terms than men. What is required, therefore, is a focus on the gendered basis of both segregation and segmentation in the labour market.

The question of segmentation has been addressed by an extension of the dual labour market theory (Barron and Norris, 1976), which sees the labour market structured into primary and secondary sectors, the former offering security, good pay and conditions, and good prospects, and the secondary sector characterized by the opposite of all these features. The argument with regard to women is that they typically occupy the jobs which are located in this secondary sector and the explanation of their position hinges partly on the assumption that they are generally more ready to accept the inferior conditions offered by such jobs. A further development of this account which sees explanation to lie with women's particular characteristics; notably poor commitment, reticence in organizing collectively, ease of identification, low inclination to train and low skill, has been much criticised (see Walby, 1986a). The profile itself may be questionable, but even if true simply raises further explanatory problems. The dual sector framework must therefore be viewed as providing at best a classificatory device for locating jobs in the structure of the labour market rather than offering an ultimate explanation for the position of any particular group.

Even accepting these limitations the theory could only be applied to an understanding of vertical (that is, hierarchical segregation) and fails to address the question of horizontal segregation (that is, the means by which women become concentrated in different areas and types of employment). Women are, for example, much more highly represented as workers in the state sector and in services than are men. One possible explanation has been the direction of women as employees into jobs which correspond to their domestic role, and hence into the caring professions, cleaning and catering, though even here the hierarchical pattern of segregation persists (see Hakim, 1979; Dex, 1985). The dual labour market theory seems to apply best, however, to manufacturing employment, and to address questions of segmentation more convincingly than segregation; the latter requiring an historical account of the means by which particular areas of work come to be viewed as essentially male or female (see, for example, Walby 1986a).

MARXIST THEORY

One explanation of segregation which relates to segmentation, has its roots in Marxist theory, and views women as a source of disadvantaged labour which can be used to undermine the pay and conditions demanded by stronger, organized (male) workers. Cockburn's account (1983) of male opposition to the introduction of new technology and female workers in the print industry provides an example of resistance to such a move. Initially, it seems, the role of female labour for capital was to break down such resistance, but women workers are also viewed by Marx as a source of cheap labour. Beechey's

(1987) explication of this position suggests that women were catered for to some degree within the family through the male wage and therefore were reckoned not to be in need of a full subsistence wage. Their wages are therefore lower because of the assumption that they are subsidized workers and provided for by a man (husband or father). As Beechey states:

It is this tendency to pay women wages below the value of labour power which is responsible for the plight of single working class women, widows and female single-parent families (p. 44)

The other aspect of Marxist theory which has been applied to the position of women is the idea of capital's need for a flexible and disposable population of workers both to depress wages and to accommodate fluctuating demand for labour. By Beechey's account married women are particularly well suited to fill such a role as they will 'disappear virtually without trace, back into the family' when their labour is no longer required. Walby has criticized this explanation of women's weak labour market position, arguing that if they offer such a cheap source of labour women would be constantly employed by capital and would thus replace men in the workforce. Following Beechey's account, however, this could not occur, since women's cheapness relies upon the assumption that they are subsidized by a male wage. If men ceased to be employed then this could not be the case. The question of the degree to which married women can in practice depend on the male wage is an empirical issue to which we will return later.

HUMAN RESOURCES

One other approach to an understanding of women's employment that should be mentioned here is the 'human capital' theory which emerges from orthodox economics. It is argued (Mincer, 1962, 1966) that women have fewer skills, experience and qualifications than men, but have a relative advantage in the domestic sphere and in child care. Men have a better command of resources in the labour market and the traditional sexual division of labour is the result. The assumption here, of course, is that workers are rewarded in proportion to their skills, a position which begs questions about the social definition of skill and the construction of jobs targeted at particular populations, neither of which are addressed by the human capital approach.

One development in the human resource field has come in the form of the 'New Home Economics' (for example, Becker, 1981) and the basic argument put forward is that in the past intrinsic differences between the sexes led, for married couples, to the comparative advantage of the man in paid employment. Recent economic change is, however, thought to be freeing individuals from traditional constraints and leaving them free to negotiate their use of time and labour in achieving the well-being of households – and yet we have already noted that women's employment position is such that they remain at a disadvantage in the labour market.

Ray Pahl's work (1984) similarly focuses on household strategies emerging from:

> The best use of resources for getting by under given social and economic conditions (p. 20)

to be later defined in the same work as:

> how households allocate their collective effort to getting all the work that they define has or feel needs to be done (p. 113)

Both these approaches suffer from taking the household as their basic unit of analysis without convincingly querying power and control over resources despite attempts in different ways to concede their limitation. It is the absence of such control that could well force married women into a labour market in which they will accept almost any conditions for the sake of some degree of financial independence. Thus their 'reserve army' role and their acceptance of less than subsistence wages could ironically be based on their minimal access to the man's wage.

The thrust of such suggestions is basically to argue that an understanding of women's position in the labour market must take account of the terms under which they enter into paid employment, both with regard to their domestic duties and to the distribution of finances within the home, as well as the nature of the opportunities available to them. What has been lacking in the perspectives briefly summarized above is any convincing theorization of the relationship between women's position in the household and their position in the labour market, though the 'reserve army' thesis perhaps comes closest. There has been a recent development which turns attention more fully to what may be termed the social construction of employment, and examines the ways in which married women are channelled into particular sorts of jobs. Before an examination of this argument it may be useful to review some of the empirical work which has bearing on the differing perspectives on women's employment, particularly with regard to changes in the UK during recession.

WOMEN AND RECESSION

Rubery and Tarling (1988) have examined women's employment in Britain during the recession of the 1970s and early 1980s, and whilst they found some evidence of the reserve army effect in certain parts of manufacturing industry and some public sector service industries, the thesis does not hold at aggregate level. Nor does there appear to have been any significant substitution of female for male workers. The major factor affecting women's rising employment has in fact been related to gender segregation in that the areas of job expansion have tended to favour jobs for women. Thus:

> Women's employment has been maintained and increased in the 1970's and early 1980's simply because those industries which have traditionally been feminized have increased their share of total employment . . .
> (p. 110)

Although there has been a gradual integration of women into most occupational sectors through the seventies the overall pattern of increase has further concentrated women in already 'feminized' sectors (p. 115). Whilst occupational segregation has reduced women's share of manufacturing employment through the 'reserve army' syndrome, it has protected and expanded their share of work in the service sector.

Rubery and Tarling suggest, however, that recent trends have been less favourable to women. Whilst women's employment in private services continued to increase as compared to men from 1981–1984, their absolute loss of public sector jobs was greater than men's such that women's jobs accounted for 85 per cent of the jobs lost in the public sector. In the private service sector women's employment continued to increase for this period but almost one-third of new jobs were in part-time work and the increase in terms of full-time equivalents was less than for men; 207 000 compared with 259 000. A pattern of part-time working may favour women in that it is the only form of employment to show overall growth but this will have implications for the terms and conditions under which many women are employed (see Chapter 2). Indeed, the lack of protection accorded to part-time and home workers has been described by Rubery and Tarling as constituting a 'legalized black economy' (p. 122).

Pollert (1988a, b) has given figures which summarize the overall change. The loss of jobs in manufacturing and the continuing growth of service sector jobs means that service industries now account for 67 per cent of total employment as compared with 59 per cent in 1979. Part-timers in the work-force grew from 21 to 23 per cent from 1981–1986 and for female employees from 42 to 46 per cent from 1981–1985. These figures, however, disguise a 40 per cent loss of women's part-time manufacturing jobs, although from 1983 job growth has been based almost exclusively on female service sector employment. Changes of this kind raise some interesting questions about the explanation for patterns of employment, and specifically the logic behind part-time employment which suggest conclusions differing from those offered by familiar theorizations of women's employment.

EXPLAINING THE CHANGE

The reserve army thesis would concentrate explanation of the creation of part-time jobs on the need for additional labour in times of expanding production, and other approaches have similarly looked to women's labour supply for an answer to part-time employment. In circumstances where labour is short, the need to construct jobs which accommodated married women's domestic obligations in order to access an untapped source of labour offers a convincing explanation of the part-time phenomenon. Robinson (1988), however, points out that when there is declining full-time employment this explanation becomes less plausible. Supply side explanations of the increase in female part-time employment are similar to explanations which give primacy to men's market work and women's domestic work. The paid employment of married women must consequently be fitted in to accommodate this schema. Viewed from the demand side, when high levels of unemployment make full-time labour easily available, these explanations fall short from the perspective of the employers.

Robinson (1988) (cf. Beechey and Perkins, 1987) has argued that it is the pattern of employers' labour requirements which provide the main reason for the employment of part-time labour. She suggests that part-time jobs exist in their own right and are not to be regarded as fractions of full-time jobs. Part-time workers are not engaged as substitutes for full-time employees in short supply. This argument challenges one aspect of the reserve army position; that part-timers are a means of accessing otherwise unavailable female workers in a shortage of labour, but corresponds to the argument that employers use part-time labour as a means of dealing with fluctuating and uncontrollable demand for products and services. The low pay which characterizes part-time work and the concentration of women in such work accentuates the segregation already apparent in men's and women's employment patterns, and further confines women to the low skilled, insecure jobs.

To accept flexibility as the sole explanation of the growth of part-time working, however, is to neglect other aspects of the advantage to employers of part-time labour. Many (though by no means all) part-time workers have weekly hours which fall below the threshold for entitlement to redundancy pay, maternity benefits and other employee rights. Although some part-time workers' hours are sufficient for them to qualify, others are excluded. The low pay of part-timers also means that there is an additional saving for employers and an additional disadvantage to the workers in that below a stated weekly threshold (currently £43) no national insurance contribution is required. As a result there is no entitlement to unemployment benefit on job loss. Thus as Robinson and Wallace (1984) argue:

> Employers preferences for part-time rather than full time labour were essential to the adoption of cost-effective employment policies dictated by pressures to improve efficiency in highly competitive conditions. (p. 396)

Though there is some evidence of substitution of part-time for full-time jobs (see Humphries and Rubery, 1988 for review) the fact of continued part-time growth when full-time labour is available indicates an employer preference for this form of employment.

WHY WOMEN?

The concentration of married women in part-time employment seems on one level to have a self evident explanation; it is a form of employment closely linked to domestic and child-care responsibilities. The Women and Employment Survey (Martin and Roberts, 1984) found that women with dependent children were more likely to work part-time than women without (35 as against 6 per cent part-time and 17 as against 78 per cent full-time), and that married women were more likely than single women to do so (33 as against 3 per cent part-time and 27 as against 79 per cent full-time). The terms upon which married women enter the labour market have been summarized by Harris and Morris (1986) as follows. Broadly speaking there are three possibilities:

1 Hours in paid employment must leave the women free at the appropriate times for the fulfilment of domestic and child-care obligations.
2 An arrangement may be made with kin or friends whereby they assume some of the domestic labour, either for financial reward or on a reciprocal basis.
3 A husband may assume a share of the activities previously defined as the responsibility of his wife.

In practice there will often be some combination of these three possibilities in order to free the woman for paid employment, but given a persistence of traditional patterns of domestic responsibility for the woman it is likely that her market labour will be constrained. It may of course be argued that with changes in employment patterns these traditional responsibilities are being broken down, both by women's paid employment and by men's unemployment, but empirical investigation has consistently shown this not to be the case (for review see Morris, 1988). Of particular interest is the finding (Gershuny et al., 1986, p. 33) that a disproportionate domestic burden falls on women employed part-time. This is partly to be explained by the fact that domestic tasks are greatest when there are young children in the home, and this is the case for most part-time workers. It is also true that while some contribution by men to domestic work is deemed appropriate if the woman works *full-time*, this is likely to be judged less necessary if her employment is part-time.

There are a number of other factors to be taken into account before accepting the 'domestic role' explanation of married women's part-time working. There is, for example, the fact that in other countries there is no comparable concentration. In the USA part-time workers make up 20 per cent of the women's labour force compared with 42 per cent in Britain (Morris, 1989). The reason for the difference is partly to be found in the British tax and National Insurance systems which have operated to make part-timers relatively cheaper, a situation which does not pertain in the USA. More advanced state recognition of child-care needs in the USA lessens one constraint on women's time and labour (Dex and Shaw, 1986), and the medical insurance attached to full-time employment only militates against any part-time preference. Beechey (1987) has made the point more generally, citing contrasts with Britain from Finland, France and Japan:

> Crossnational evidence makes it clear that there is no simple correlation between female activity rates and part time working (p. 41)

There is also evidence from the UK which suggests that domestic factors can be overridden where financial need is sufficiently strong. Bruegel (1988), for example, has found that black women (that is, West Indian and Asian) are more likely to be economically active and less likely to work part-time than white women. Her argument is that this difference can be explained by different economic pressures as black households rely more heavily on women's income. This need can, however, be secondary where there is a forceful cultural opposition to women's employment, as is the case among Moslem Asian women (Stone, 1983).

THE SOCIAL CONSTRUCTION OF EMPLOYMENT

Whilst the evidence about domestic and child-care constraints is compelling it is clearly only one contributory factor in the explanation of British women's part-time employment. Beechey (1987) has examined some of the prevailing theoretical approaches to part-time work such as: 'some types of work lend themselves by their nature to part-time employment' (Myrdal and Klein, 1956) and has criticized over-attention to supply side explanations which give primacy to women's domestic obligations such that women are deemed to be naturally suited to certain kinds of employment. Her suggestion is that the factors associated with the use of part-time labour; flexibility, covering for breaks, extending the working day, only resulted in jobs being organized on a part-time basis when women were employed. Other mechanisms were used when the workers were men. Beechey provides two interesting examples from a study of part-time work in Coventry (Beechey and Perkins, 1987). Hospital portering was found to be an exclusively male occupation, and though there were factors operating (for instance the need for 24 hour cover) which would normally suggest an argument for part-time work they were dealt with by shift work rather than part-time employment. Another example was bread production where casual labour and shift work were used to provide flexibility. The conclusion suggested (Beechey, 1987, p. 164) is that:

> A crucial part of the explanation as to why certain jobs are part time is that they are typically done by women, and that the demand for part time labour is inextricably linked to the presence of occupational segregation. (p. 164)

There is also at least a suggestion that part-time jobs are by definition regarded as unskilled, 'even when they involve complex competencies and responsibilities' (Beechey and Perkins, 1987, p. 29), or as others have argued (Phillips and Taylor 1980, p. 55) 'skill definitions are saturated with sexual bias'. A weakened position is particularly likely to come about with a work-force physically fragmented, as part-timers often are, and short of time, as mothers of young children often are, which inevitably makes their availability for full-time employment difficult to organize.

There is also a literature concerned to identify the processes by which gender plays a role in recruitment which serves to channel men and women towards the jobs which are deemed appropriate (Curran, 1988). This development strengthens Beechey's point (1987, p. 166) that whilst it is possible to separate supply and demand analytically, in practice they are highly interdependent; women limit their job choice to what they expect to be available, whilst employers construct jobs to take advantage of a vulnerable section of the work-force whose perceived options are limited. In the case of part-time work we have seen that this doubly suits employers because of the financial incentive. Thus:

> The demand for particular kinds of labour may depend less upon some actual supply of labour than upon managements' perceptions of what kinds of labour are available, and what work is appropriate for married women or married women with dependants. (Beechey, 1987, p. 166)

PERCEPTIONS OF GENDER ROLES

Arguably ideological constructions will affect the nature of jobs available to different sections of the work-force, as well as the incumbant's perceptions of their own potential. These ideological constructions will also have some bearing on the sexual division of labour in the home in that they affect the way that women's employment is perceived. A full understanding of this dynamic, however, first requires some examination of the 'principal earner' fallacy.

Supplementary benefit regulations, now superseded by Income Support, grew out of a particular economic arrangement, and an associated ideology which seemed to indicate reliance of the nuclear family household upon a male wage. A related assumption was the dependent status of the woman, and the man was consequently deemed to be the appropriate applicant for benefit. His wife's earnings, if she had any, were calculated as part of his income in assessing his claim. In other words, a particular kind of model for the organization of domestic life eventually found expression and support in the early formulation of much social policy. This argument has been clearly documented by a number of writers (see Land, 1976; Lewis, 1982).

One of the assumptions upon which the welfare state in Britain was founded was that marriage removed women from the labour market, and properly so. It became the legal and moral duty of a husband to support his wife, with both state insurance and benefit provisions acknowledging the man as provider. It was thus, presumably in dismay, that Beveridge observed in 1951:

> It is a remarkable thing that in the so-called welfare state there are more married women aged 25 to 55 at work outside the home than in any peace time year during the past half century. (quoted in Young, 1952)

It is now possible for either partner in a married couple to claim benefit on behalf of the household, but though this may produce a change in the identity of the claimant, the employment effects will be unchanged. A claimant, regardless of gender is allowed an additional income of only £5 a week, except in cases of long-term unemployment, where a couples' joint additional income may be £15. Given that a woman's wage, especially if she is in part-time employment, is unlikely to exceed benefit levels, there has been a strong disincentive against her taking on, or continuing in, employment if the household is claiming.

The advantageous rate for the long-term unemployed was introduced only a year ago and it remains to be seen whether this will remove the disincentive. So far, it has certainly been the case that a husband's employment status will very strongly influence that of his wife. In some cases this has meant a woman will leave her own job in response to unemployment for the man. In other cases a calculated decision may be made about the probability of the man finding further employment. We should remember here that a higher disregard of the wife's earnings will apply while the man is claiming unemployment benefit. Thus in cases of periodic employment or short-term contracts for the man, the argument in favour of the woman retaining her job is stronger especially since she could not guarantee to find her way back into work if she relinquished the current job – though factors such as male pride may intervene.

The 'benefit effect' is not, in practice, the only factor influencing married women's employment decisions in cases of male unemployment, and Joshi (1984) has identified a number of other influences: a couple may wish to share more time together, the woman may experience an increased domestic load due to the man's presence in the home, and there may be a reluctance on her part to usurp the breadwinner role. The end result in terms of the pattern of employment is that there are no-earner couples in which both the man and woman are out of employment, couples in which the woman remains in employment throughout the man's short-term spells out of work, and relatively consistently and securely employed couples with both the man and the woman holding jobs. In a majority of the latter cases the woman's employment will be to some degree motivated either by the overall inadequacy of the man's wage or by the inadequacy of the amount she receives to cover domestic needs; as well as the social rewards of employment outside the home.

Because of the way in which household finances are often organized (for review see Morris with Ruane, 1989) the woman's need for additional money may not be perceived by her husband. This is certainly the case where her wage is absorbed into the housekeeping money; the most common use to which married women's earnings are put (Morris, 1989; Morris with Ruane, 1989). Thus many households become dependent on women's earnings in a way which is not perceived as a challenge to established gender roles. The woman who works part-time when her husband is employed is 'supplementing' her housekeeping, whilst in homes where the man is out of work the woman is most likely to continue in her job if his unemployment is perceived as being temporary. Thus his essential breadwinner role remains unchallenged.

WOMEN'S EMPLOYMENT AND HOUSEHOLD FINANCE

Early attempts to predict the labour market behaviour of married women were based upon spouses income. Although the more sophisticated of these models corrected a bias which tested only the effect of the man's wage on the woman and built in a possible two-way effect (for review see Brown, 1983), the problem remained that labour supply predictions based on the earnings of a spouse depend upon the uses of, benefits from and access to, that income. We referred earlier to the work of Becker and its contribution towards formulating a 'New Household Economics'. Becker's advance (1981) was to use the household as the focus for analysis, whilst conceding the possibility of 'shirking, pilfering and other malfeasance' (p. 32). In his thesis the household is self-balancing; if selfishness to maximize personal income produces a reduction in contribution from the altruist then behaviour will be amended to maximize household income in self-interest.

Women's employment is an interesting instance of the difficulty of applying this thesis, partly because of gendered responsibilities and spending patterns. Thus, in cases of male 'selfishness' (that is, withholding income from housekeeping for personal reasons), the response of the woman is often to *increase* her contribution by entering the labour market to augment an inadequate allowance. Here the man's power over his own earned income and his control over her access to it drives her not to withdraw her own contribution to domestic services, but to make up the financial shortfall with her own paid labour. Gendered spending responsibilities seem to lead her in these circumstances to dedicate her income to household spending. Such conclusions raise questions about the validity of approaching married women's labour supply through a consideration of overall household income, rather than directing attention towards women's motivation in seeking employment, and their distinctive pattern of spending.

The point has often been made that the number of households in poverty would increase fourfold without the contribution of married women's earnings (see for example McLennan, Pond and Sullivan, 1983), and research has shown that the earnings of women are most critical when they account for a relatively low level of household income. Thus Martin and Roberts (1984) found that women contributing 30 per cent and over were *less* likely to say that they could not manage financially without their earnings than women contributing 20 per cent and less. A low proportional contribution to total household income is of course made likely by the concentration of married women in part-time employment, whilst this pattern is in turn related to child-care constraints. As we have noted this has encouraged some husbands to perceive their wife's employment as in some way secondary and not strictly 'necessary'; a view which contrasts with many women's perceptions of their earnings.

There is a wealth of literature which indicates that by far the commonest use of married women's earnings is on household and child related spending (see Rimmer, 1980; Land, 1981; Cragg and Dawson, 1984) although this, somewhat confusingly, is seen as conferring independence. An example of this confusion is reported in research findings from the north east of England (Morris, 1987) where women talk of borrowing from husbands to meet the demands of the household, and equate financial independence with an ability to supplement the housekeeping money (cf. Cragg and Dawson, 1981). The explanation of this dedication of women's earnings to household spending seems to lie in the pattern of gendered responsibilities to emerge from a traditional sexual division of labour which associates the woman with the running of the home, and which seems to be substantially unchallenged.

HOMEWORKING

A particular instance of the way in which women's economic role can be tied to their unpaid domestic role is through homeworking, whereby the primacy of the domestic role constrains even the location of paid work. There are problems related both to definition and data collection which have been well reviewed by Allen and Wolkowitz (1987). They argue that official estimates appear to substantially underestimate the incidence of homeworking, and have often accepted an unrealistically broad category of 'home-based work'. Thus:

By using the notion of home-based work official records and estimates blur the differences between petty commodity producers, small scale entrepreneurs and self-employed artisans and waged workers. (p. 51)

It is therefore unsurprising that the working conditions and earning capacity of those classified as homeworkers vary enormously. The breadth of the definition, however, yields some interesting findings in the Department of Employment study of home-based work (Hakim, 1987, p. 241–242). For example, the majority of homeworkers (71 per cent) are women whilst the majority of people working from home as a base (71 per cent) are men. Hakim's study also shows that they are among the highest paid workers in Britain (one-fifth with hourly earnings in the top 10 per cent) and among the lowest paid (one-third with hourly earnings in the lowest 10 per cent), however the great majority of workers in the former category are men and in the latter category women; three quarters of homeworkers are satisfied with their pay, but ironically women are more satisfied than men.

A more narrowly defined study of homeworking in wages council industries (Hakim and Dennis, 1982) reports some interesting data on child-care responsibility. References to children were given frequently as an indication of domestic responsibilities which might hinder efficient working methods at home, lowering output and earnings. A substantial number of homeworkers, though by no means all, seemed likely to be influenced by the presence of children in their acceptance of homework; two-thirds of those aged 20–39 years and one-quarter of those aged 40–59 years had children at home. Another 2 per cent of the younger group and 4 per cent of the older group had an elderly relative to care for. Those with children were also the only group working longer than the average hours for all homeworkers and longer hours than those with other reasons for working at home. Hakim and Dennis attribute this pattern to the financial burden of children and the consequent need for extra income. It may also be related to the number of interruptions experienced, which would keep productivity and therefore pay down without additional hours of work. An earlier qualitative study (Cragg and Dawson, 1981, p. 6–8) found dependent children to be overwhelmingly the main reason for working at home with additional factors including ill health, language and cultural reasons.

Using data collected in four areas of West Yorkshire, Allen and Wolkowitz (1987) confirm some of the findings of the official studies but challenge others. They make the point, for example, that child-care responsibilities do not differ sharply between homeworkers and other women workers (p. 73). Whilst conceding that responsibility for children is one of the ideological constraints which shape women's paid employment they claim that this emphasis obscures women's other family responsibilities, making it appear as if the limits on women's waged labour are confined to a single stage in the domestic cycle when clearly they are not. The need to fit in work with the care of a husband and the husband's child-care preferences were also noted as factors influencing women's employment choice.

As with the Department of Employment reports, Allen and Wolkowitz stress the importance of earnings for essential budgetary items such as food, heating, lighting, rent or mortgage, rates and shoes and clothes for children though as we noted of other research on women's paid work the subsistence factor was often intertwined with the desire for a degree of independence (p. 70–71). Again echoing research findings on women's paid work more generally they found that the highest proportionate contributions to household income were at the lowest end of the income scale, but that nevertheless even women whose husbands were comparatively well paid also made significant contributions to household income.

Allen and Wolkowitz treat with caution the idea that immigrant workers kept home by language problems or illegal status form a major part of the homework labour force. As with the 'dependent children' argument this ignores the participation of women with the same characteristics in work outside the home, though they concede the *possibility* (p. 82) that Pakistani women, for example, could be subject to stronger patriarchal controls than other groups might be. Such explanations are deemed to be 'not so much fallacious as inadequate' for:

> Homeworkers are not exceptional or atypical in their requirements or circumstances . . . (but) . . . Homeworking is a particularly appalling example of women's position in the labour market, not a contrast to it. (p. 85)

CONCLUSION

This chapter has examined those aspects of women's employment which most clearly demonstrate the nature of their disadvantage in the labour market. In this context most notable are the increasing incidence of married women in part-time work, and their disproportionate presence in the least satisfactory instances of homeworking. Whilst these phenomena by no means exhaust the range of women's employment they do constitute the most obvious examples of women's 'poor work', and can most readily be understood by an examination of that other aspect of ill-rewarded labour, women's domestic work.

However, one major source of dissatisfaction with established theoretical accounts of women's labour market position has been that they concentrate to an unacceptable degree on the characteristics and/or conditions of labour supply, that is on the women themselves, and insufficiently on the nature of the demand for their labour. The strength of a supply side orientation is that it highlights – for married women particularly – the constraining effect of domestic and child-care obligations. Whilst any inclination to view these constraints as natural or absolutely determining has been strongly criticized, so too have over-optimistic accounts of the potential for a renegotiation of domestic roles. Recent empirical research has shown few grounds for such optimism.

Nevertheless, in understanding the implications of women's domestic role for their labour market position it has become increasingly important to focus attention on employers' attitudes to and perceptions of women workers, on gendered processes of selection and recruitment, and on the very construction of the jobs to be filled. Part-time work has received a good deal of attention in this context, not least because of its significant growth in recent years, though homeworking has been relatively neglected.

The emerging perspective is one which examines the interaction between women's domestic circumstances, their ideological underpinnings, the social construction of employment and the statutory framework in which this operates, as well as the detail of financial arrangements within the home. This complex of factors is the key to explaining the continuing availability of married women for poor work, at low pay, under inferior conditions of employment, and the incentive to employers to continue to recruit them. The Labour Force Survey (1989) findings for 1988 do, however, indicate some slowing of the pace of change and some shifts in direction.

Between 1985 and 1987 the numbers in full-time employment had been declining, whilst part-time employment for women showed particularly strong growth. Whilst the growth was maintained between 1987 and 1988 it has been more marked for men than in previous years, although this still leaves them far behind married women: 569 000 employees in contrast to 3 547 000. At the same time full-time employment has begun to recover, with 60 per cent of the growth for 1987–1988 being in full-time work. These results do not, however, necessarily presage any change in the associations which have been discussed in this chapter. The argument has been that the domestic circumstances of married women, together with employers' gendered perceptions of what constitutes an appropriate employment pattern have so far conspired to produce and perpetuate the part-time female phenomenon. The same would be true of aspects of the market for homeworkers.

Any change in circumstances would require:

1 A fall in demand for such employment, which seems unlikely in the immediate future.
2 A change in employers' perceptions of appropriate labour, which may have begun but which as yet, has far to go.
3 A shift in domestic arrangements such that women had less motivation for entering employment, or were less constrained in the nature of their employment by domestic and child-care obligations.

There has been some moderate growth in part-time employment for men, which suggests that employers' attitudes may be changing, and data cited above show some evidence of increased male domestic involvement. The extent of this change has not yet been sufficient to redress the concentration of married women as the principal part-time work-force, or to lift their responsibility as principal domestic workers and carers. Until such a move has taken place it is unlikely that constraints on their paid work will be loosened, or that employers perceptions of appropriate work-force patterns will be significantly challenged.

6

Poor work and poor institutions: training and the youth labour market

DAVID LEE

INTRODUCTION

Young workers are especially vulnerable to 'poor work'. They are excluded by their very youth from many of the more attractive sectors of the labour market and are especially vulnerable to fluctuations in the general level of labour demand. Those with little experience or training to offer are especially at risk of being used as cheap labour on low skilled exploitative tasks. Furthermore, changes in the wider pattern of employment have restricted the range of job openings available to such youths. Were it not for the somewhat uncertain impact of demographic factors, which have reduced the total numbers of young adults seeking jobs for the first time, the problem for the least academically successful would in future not simply be one of 'poor work' but whether they will be able to find work at all. Theoretically, young workers' vulnerability can be offset by legislation and institutional control over the early years of work, for example, through state regulated training programmes. But whether or not the forces of the market are effectively constrained in this way varies from one industrial society to another, according to the prevailing industrial relations climate and political culture.

This chapter begins with a general discussion of young people's position in the labour market. It argues that institutional as well as economic causes make them vulnerable to job insecurity, low pay, and exploitative working conditions which constitute poor work. It then considers how governments have responded to the particularly insecure conditions facing young workers in the recent past. After a brief discussion of West Germany, which is often held up as a model for Britain to follow, the remainder of the chapter tries to analyse the contrast with British practice, both historically and under the

Conservative governments of the eighties. The conclusion considers the implications for future policy.

ECONOMIC FACTORS IN THE VULNERABILITY OF YOUNG WORKERS TO POOR WORK

The economics of the youth labour market became a matter of academic and political controversy in many Western societies in the early eighties because of rising levels of youth joblessness. In Britain the most informative debate was about whether the collapse in youth employment was caused by 'structural' or 'cyclical' factors. The so-called structuralist position argued that 'young people's disadvantaged position in the labour market was due to the concentration of the jobs available to them in a limited number of occupational and industrial orders'. Because these industries and occupations were now declining, school leavers faced a long-term and permanent deterioration in employment prospects and job quality (Ashton and Maguire, 1986). The cyclical position challenged the evidence for this prognosis and questioned whether a separate youth labour market existed. The current crisis had arisen, it was argued, because youth labour is particularly sensitive to fluctuations in the general level of demand. The intake of new labour dries up in a recession, and also young workers already employed are often the first to be laid off. This explains why young people have formed a disproportionately large part of the total unemployed. The effect is more pronounced among young females than young males. But conversely, youth employment recovers faster than adult employment as the economy as a whole revives (Raffe, 1986).

Although this debate was important in showing the complexity of the factors which shape the lives of young workers, it is now largely superseded. More recent research shows that youth unemployment has resulted from a mixture of both structural and cyclical causes of which not the least important are permanent changes in global markets and the labour policies of multinational companies. Cyclical theories work best when applied to jobs offering training. In Britain and elsewhere large firms cut back their training places and labour overheads during the recession of the early eighties. Insecure, low skill work simultaneously became more widespread, because hiring young workers and 'trainees' on low wages offered a means by which more marginal (mostly smaller) firms might survive (Roberts, Dench and Richardson, 1986; Casey, 1986; Ashton, Maguire and Spilsbury, 1990).

Structural theories are better at explaining the distribution of youth employment and identifying factors which tend to make young workers into a separate labour force restricted to poor work. Recent comparative research found that industries which employ a relatively large proportion of young people either have low overall wage rates or youth wage rates which are low relative to their prevailing adult pay levels (Marsden and Ryan, 1988a,

Chapter 2). However, pay levels partly depend on variations between different types of industry in the importance of labour costs as a proportion of total outlay. In Britain, youth labour is concentrated in labour intensive manufacturing and in the service trades (which are also highly labour intensive). Small firm industries tend to be low paying industries too, so that a relatively large number of young people work in small firms. Good up-to-date evidence is hard to come by, but it seems that the concentration of young people in low wage employment is found in most advanced industrial societies and in some cases is even more marked than in Britain. Furthermore, until the end of the 1970s the pattern had been stable for at least 20 years and probably longer.

The crux of the problem is that unless youth labour was relatively cheap few employers would have any commercial reason to employ youths instead of adults. Young workers needing training or work experience have had to take the less attractive and poorest paid jobs until they became qualified or old enough to enter the longer term jobs filled exclusively by adults. It is important to acknowledge that apprenticeships and similar low paid jobs for young people have until now acted as 'staging posts' to better paid work (Marsden and Ryan, 1988a, 3.5). But it is also generally the case that *low wage industries* have fewer realistic training opportunities and career prospects and indeed in the worst cases the jobs are dead end and insecure. Furthermore, the problem of 'blind alley jobs' is, too often, closely linked to the problem of youth joblessness. Although there is always a hard core of young people who have been out of work for a long time, many unemployed youngsters tend to alternate periods of unemployment with a succession of insecure jobs. Even in boom conditions, insecurity of tenure is a factor that can make jobs poor in quality. The young people recruited to them tend to drift from one job to the next and to become trapped by their continuing lack of training in a low wage (or 'secondary') sector of the youth labour market.

Worse, in Britain at least, changes in the overall structure of employment do appear to be increasing the relative size of this low paid secondary sector. Throughout the post-war period, manufacturing employment has been declining because of technical change and increasingly competitive product markets. By the recession of the early eighties, the national markets for products and labour had become incorporated into a global economy dominated by the volatile decisions of multinational companies. The recession intensified these trends. Manufacturing employment fell from 7 million in 1979 to 5 million in 1987. At the same time, employment in the service sector rose from just over 13 million to 14.5 million. The decline of manufacturing has meant fewer traineeships, apprenticeships and other 'staging posts' for young workers. The rise of the service trades with their relatively lower wages, fewer traineeships and limited career structures implies that young people will in future be more likely to find themselves permanently trapped in 'poor work'. (See Ashton, Maguire and Spilsbury, 1990, Chapter 2 for an extensive discussion). Alternatively, the most serious economic effects of any demographically caused shortage of young workers will be in the industries which were always 'heavy users' of cheap youth labour.

Young people's lives appear to be growing much more polarized. On the one hand more are staying on at school or college and entering the growing number of jobs requiring extended education, while on the other hand the remainder are increasingly deskilled and restricted to semi-skilled and 'blind alley' jobs – or no jobs at all. The problem would by now be extremely serious were it not for the current decline in the absolute size of the age group itself (Department of Employment, 1988a).

INSTITUTIONAL FACTORS IN THE VULNERABILITY OF YOUNG PEOPLE TO POOR WORK

Clearly, then, cyclical and structural changes in economic activity are not entirely distinct. Both can and do affect young people's working lives and future prospects. However, there is also a range of non-economic or 'institutional' influences which have to be considered, not least because they underlie and determine how the so-called 'forces of the market' themselves behave (Maurice, Sellier and Silvestre, 1986; Marsden, 1986). To illustrate, we shall look at: (a) the varying link between national systems of schooling and employment; (b) the different 'pay regimes' which young workers encounter in different societies; and (c) the segmentation of the market itself.

School and employment

Main-stream economists treat education as an investment in what they call 'human capital' with much the same consequences wherever it is made. Young people who extend their education are in effect deferring their earning to learn skills which enable them to avoid the less attractive sectors of the youth labour market. Likewise those who accept low wages while training eventually expect to enter work at an advantageous point on an established career track. In fact, in most industrial societies the numbers extending their education have risen in recent years and the vulnerability of these individuals to poor work remains relatively low compared with those who, for whatever reason, 'fail' at school.

Yet these same societies still differ greatly in the average years of schooling which pupils receive and in the proportion who drop out early and become vulnerable to sub-standard employment. They also vary in the qualitative aspects of schooling, especially in the extent to which the school system sets out to prepare pupils for work and what degree of prestige or stigma is attached to vocational as compared to academic studies. Also, many young people leave full-time schooling to seek training in employment, yet the relationship between education and training within employment also varies from society to society as we shall see below. Thus although 'investment in human capital' may reduce young people's liability to 'poor work', cultural and political differences in the transition to the labour market make a major difference to how well the market recognizes and uses human capital.

Even education and training can sometimes still lead young people into poor work. Students are often an important casual labour force, obliged to undertake menial part-time work in order to finance their studies. A more serious problem arises when there are insufficient jobs to absorb all of the qualified labour. It has been claimed that in third world societies especially the ensuing diploma disease (Dore, 1976) condemns many well qualified individuals to work that is poor relative to their expectations. Even in advanced societies such as the USA and France credentials may be too academic or not matched to the existing demand for skills, so creating an 'overqualification' problem (Ben-David, 1966; Freeman, 1976) again showing the limitations of a purely economic human capital approach.

Pay regimes

The cultural and political factors which shape educational systems also lead to marked differences in so-called 'pay regimes' between countries (Marsden and Ryan, 1988a, b). Pay regimes are sets of rules which modify, and in some cases completely override market influences on wage levels. Collective bargaining and union strategies are a major source of such rules, especially where cheap youth labour acts as a possible threat to adult jobs. The conditions of youth employment and, indeed, collective bargaining itself, may also be regulated by state legislation. The significance of these regulatory variations can be illustrated by comparing, France, Germany and Britain. In France, fixed rates for the job typically allow little or no reduction for youth or trainee status. This tends to restrict young people to a narrow range of jobs in mainly small firms which cannot compete with the wage rates of larger corporations. Widespread use of apprenticeship in Britain and Germany has resulted in a framework of 'wage for age' rules which makes young people attractive to a greater range of employers. However, British employers have tended to use wage for age rules to undercut adult employment, a policy which has soured industrial relations and led unions to attempt to raise youth relative wages (Ryan, 1986; Lee, 1989). In Germany, unions accept very low apprentice wage rates in return for statutory controls on training programmes and on the use of youth labour (Marsden and Ryan, 1988a; Streeck *et al.*, 1987).

Labour market segmentation

The youth labour market, once entered, is 'segmented', that is rigidified by barriers which prevent movement of certain classes of worker between areas of poor or more attractive employment, with pay often varying widely over similar kinds of work. So-called 'institutional' factors are mainly responsible for these rigidities. They include the institutional pay regimes already mentioned and the devices which trade unions, especially in Britain, use to limit the amount of cheap youth labour taken on.

In describing labour market segmentation it is helpful to distinguish between the rigidities which affect workers even before they enter the labour market (called *pre-market* segmentation) from those which emerge within the market itself (called *in-market* segmentation) (Ryan, 1981).

One of the most important causes of pre-market segmentation are gender divisions. Although girls do not necessarily drop out of education more than boys (as they did in the past) there is still in most countries a noticeable segregation in the kinds of occupations entered by males and females. In Britain the range of female employment remains restricted and poorly paid relative to men's with poorer job security and less training (Wickham, 1986; Ashton and Maguire, 1986; Walby, 1989). Thus the meaning of poor work for young people is segregated qualitatively along gender lines, with young women often very vulnerable to employment in unsatisfactory trades and industries.

Equally important are the differentiating effects of ethnic and social class background, not least because from the earliest years of children's lives, social background is strongly related to patterns of educational achievement or under-achievement (see for example, Burgess, 1986; Chapters 4 and 5). In turn educational differences lead to marked segregation of the entry points to occupations. But educational credentials are used to screen applicants for personality and background characteristics that are thought to make for trainability and potential reliability as employees, rather than for their human capital input. Ashton and Maguire (1986), for example, have identified four such different occupational entry levels which, when combined with the effects of gender gives no less than eight broad pre-market segments within the British youth labour market.

Lastly, there are the 'in-market' aspects of youth employment which cause some young people to be trapped in poor work and often cut across pre-market influences. Geographical variation in the local industry mix and employment levels are a major example. In a study of youth labour markets in three separate British localities Ashton and Maguire found that employment chances of middle-class youths in one locality were worse than for working-class youths in another (Ashton and Maguire, 1986). Such effects arise because locality is a serious restriction on the mobility of young people between better and worse jobs. Young people who do not go in for extended study are especially dependent on what is available in their immediate locality for they tend to lack either the money or the means to move to job markets elsewhere.

Equally important are employer recruitment and training policies. Arguably only the least skilled jobs, with the poorest conditions recruit through open wage competition and as we have already noted, once young people enter this sector they may find it difficult to get out again. Large employers tend to develop so-called 'internal' labour markets, retaining valued workers by incorporating their training, pay and conditions into regulated promotion chains which can only be entered at specific entry points. Where apprenticed crafts exist, workers are trained in transferable skills and only then do they have the possibility of transfer between different employers.

The relative significance of internal, occupational or competitive youth labour markets can be shown to depend greatly on the all important role of state policy in framing the way labour market institutions develop and interact. And as our discussion of education suggested, this in turn will depend on the cultural and political history of each industrial society. Comparing different industrialized nation states shows that some state policies have made young people far more vulnerable to poor work than others. So in order to put our discussion into some kind of comparative context we shall briefly contrast the situation in Britain with that in West Germany.

WEST GERMAN YOUTH AND THE REGULATION OF EMPLOYMENT

Unique historical factors account for the distinctive route taken by German labour market institutions. The trauma of the second world war and reconstruction in a context of cold war politics encouraged political moderation and the building of a bargained consensus between capital and labour. The institutional roots of this consensus, though, go back further through the Weimar Republic and to Bismark's attempts to incorporate the late nineteenth century working class through vocational training and paternalism in the workplace. These kept the mass of the people out of academic education and instead provided them with schools which prepared them for practical duty in the workplace. Despite recent reforms, education in the Federal Republic of Germany (FRG) still remains deeply affected by this legacy of rigid social class stratification (Musgrave, 1970; Williamson, 1979).

Yet there is now a substantial body of literature suggesting that the way young people are trained and socialized into the world of work is one important condition of the vibrant performance of West German business (recent examples are Prais, 1981; Maurice, Sellier and Silvestre, 1986; Wagner, 1986). The hard distinction, and mutual recrimination, between the educational and industrial worlds familiar in the British context is far less evident in the FRG. State guidelines for the schools attended by the less academic majority stipulate that as much as one-third of the secondary curriculum should be taken up with work preparation lessons. In contrast, the school systems of France and Britain have tended to make all pupils attempt an academic curriculum and it is success or failure in this strict academic sense which shapes subsequent work histories. To take up vocational studies is too often stigmatizing, a sign of relative failure (Maurice, Sellier and Silvestre, 1986). In contrast it is usual even for very talented young West Germans to undertake vocational studies, which are arranged to form a progression which can, if necessary, lead back into a more academic curriculum or into higher education (Maurice, Sellier and Silvestre, 1986; Streeck et al., 1987). Of course, in Britain schools have recently been obliged under the so-called New Vocationalism of the eighties to adopt work relevant curricula and to increase their links with industry. The influence of industry and business over what goes on in schools have been deliberately increased. Yet big differences with German practice remain, not least being that industry oriented education is prestigious and co-exists with much more education oriented industry.

In the FRG, company law has long required firms to register with one of the statutory Chambers of Trade as a condition of being allowed to operate at all. These chambers obliged their members to provide the maximum possible range of apprenticeships and to train to specified standards. Apprenticeship has become a sought after route from school to work and covers some 90 per cent of school leavers. These days the function of setting apprentice training standards has been taken over by agencies of the federal and regional state which include representatives of both employers and unions. Skill standards, training programmes and training personnel and supervisory staff all have to be monitored and formally assessed according to external standards set by these multi-party bodies. The individual firm has little choice in principle but to observe them. Pressure to maintain standards and use them in the interests of the individual workers rather than firms comes from the system of worker–management workplace co-determination which prevails in the larger units of West German industry. Because of these formal institutional controls on the labour market, unions in the FRG have not attempted to control, restrict or demarcate job structures. They have been willing to allow skills to be modified and apprentices to receive relatively low wage rates. The result has been that there are more training opportunities in a wider range of firms and industries, and relatively fewer young people are recruited into unregulated work or become unemployed.

The West German apprenticeship system still has serious defects. Its critics claim that enforcement of training standards has been a longstanding problem and so has the misuse of apprenticeship to mask 'poor work' (Reubens, 1973). There is a danger of training syllabuses becoming too rigid and many young people, on completion of their apprenticeship, do not take up work in the area for which they have been trained (Herget, 1986). Under conditions of economic recession the quantity of training places has been maintained but arguably this has been achieved with some loss of quality. Also, the system may merely postpone youth unemployment to the age of completion of apprenticeship (Casey, 1986). Apprenticeship works out unfavourably for girls and for the children of immigrant workers who form an important and severely disadvantaged minority in West German society (Schweikert, 1982).

Nevertheless, the labour policies of West German industry and business have clearly been moved by law toward the notion of 'institutionally enforced social obligations' (Streeck, 1989) not least in relation to the treatment of the bulk of young people. The next section argues that this is the essential contrast with British practice.

POOR WORK AND THE BRITISH YOUTH

In Britain the idea that employers and firms should be obliged to put specified social obligations before commercial interest has run contrary to state policy. This has been dominated by *laissez-faire* and neo-liberal influences which the so-called Keynsian welfare consensus of the post-war period only temporarily and imperfectly interrupted. Moreover, many employers have been engaged in a battle with the trade union movement (and at times with the state itself) over the principle of 'managements right to manage', which on the whole they have successfully defended.

Victorian *laissez-faire* sought to restrict the role of the state to the encouragement of voluntary initiative and individual bargaining. In the twentieth century those in politics who sought to enforce social obligations on individuals or groups through state actions have had to struggle against the continuing legacy of *laissez-faire*, and against the complacency and the administrative inertia it fostered. For example, statements by Governments and civil servants have repeatedly insisted that youth training was primarily the responsibility of industry itself not the state. This 'pragmatic tradition of voluntarism' has persisted throughout the twentieth century even though it has become increasingly obvious that the quantity and quality of skills training is falling behind that of the country's main competitors (Sheldrake and Vickerstaff, 1987). The standard response to the problem has been further exhortation and appeals to employers' self-interest, rather than any insistence that training should be treated as a social obligation.

In fact, it is very unlikely that young people can be trained to a standard adequate for either their own or the economy's needs simply by relying on the self-interest of firms and employers. For industry, training is a cost. The greater the skill the more time and money must be spent and many firms are unwilling or unable to absorb these costs unless they can see a relatively short-term pay-off to themselves – or unless the non-market inducements to train as a social obligation are very powerful (Lindley, 1983; Chapman and Tooze, 1987; Lee *et al.*, 1990, chp. 2).

The result is that poor work for young people has been a persistent feature of the British economy right up to the present time (Roberts, 1984). Training opportunities have been largely restricted to male dominated apprenticeships in traditional crafts and as we shall see, even apprenticeship training itself has become outmoded, opportunities and facilities being circumscribed by employer self-interest and union restrictions. Outside of apprenticeship very few school leavers have received any further training at all. Recurrent crises in the supply of skilled labour have co-existed with a relatively high proportion of untrained young people who were vulnerable to low wages in exploitative, insecure jobs. What was called the 'boy labour' problem in Victorian times – the large numbers of young people wasted in exploitative low skill work – became a recurrent theme of social commentators in the twenties and regularly provoked demands for more direct and positive state funding and provision of training. The plea has typically fallen on deaf political ears. Governments have been forced to respond to the poor condition of young workers and the young unemployed at times, especially during slumps and war time. But typically such intervention has been treated as a temporary emergency measure until industry was 'on its feet' again (Sheldrake and Vickerstaff, 1987).

True, bolder measures have occasionally been adopted but only to falter because of lack of enforcement and political lobbying from opposed vested interests, especially employers dependent on cheap youth labour. For example, under the Fisher Education Act of 1918 young workers were to be compulsorily released for Day Continuation Classes but the relevant clauses were never implemented because 'industry' argued the post-war depression made the plan too costly. Under the 1944 Education Act Local Education Authorities were to establish County Colleges for the same purpose, but again the plan met resistance and was never implemented. The 1964 Industrial Training Act obliged firms to pay a training levy to an Industry Training Board if they were not providing training to a given standard. Again pressure from the lobby representing small firms resulted in the virtual abolition in 1973 of the levy grant system (Perry, 1976).

Laissez-faire policies at state level have thus in turn encouraged employers in the belief that they had a right to run their workplaces as they saw fit. Recognizing a social obligation to labour, and especially to young workers, was literally 'none of their business' and as social historians such as Barnett have argued, over time this has had profoundly negative consequences for the attitudes and commitment of the British working class (Barnett, 1986, chp. 12). Lack of training and education and a reluctance to discuss 'trade secrets' with workmen has fostered an anti-learning culture. A basically calculative attitude to labour management produces low trust, conflict-ridden industrial relations (Fox, 1974). Apprenticeship and youth wages were among the more intractable issues around which industrial conflict in Britain revolved. The causes partly lay in the occupational union organization of the skilled craft workers which encouraged them to restrict the supply of new recruits to keep up wages. However, the problem was intensified by the deskilling and mechanization of craft trades in engineering and elsewhere from the late nineteenth century onward. Apprenticeship and manning controls became key means through which the craftsmen tried to

defend their position. Employers responded, wherever possible, by formaliz-
ing in collective agreements the concept of 'managements right to manage'.

The issue might have been resolved satisfactorily by state measures to
retrain the redundant craftsmen and insure them against unemployment.
Arguably, too, the industrial relations problems associated with apprenticeship were and are a symptom, rather than a cause, of the underlying
reluctance of employers to have their use of apprentice and trainee labour
externally monitored and supervised (Lee, 1979). For example, the lack of
Governmental intervention in training allowed many employers during the
inter-war period to use 'apprentices' with impunity as cheap labour (Ryan,
1986). So in the post-war period, unions insisted on rigidifying their controls
over entry to skilled trades or failing that to raise all youth wages including
that of apprentices. Consequently, even today, apprentice pay in Britain is
relatively higher than in Germany and this strengthens the disincentive to
individual firms to create training places and facilities. It is this background
which has affected the nature and outcome of the measures adopted by the
Thatcher Government to deal with the crisis which befell the British youth
labour market in the 1980s.

'SURROGATE' LABOUR MARKETS AND POOR WORK IN THE EIGHTIES

Economic conditions in the early eighties obliged a number of Western
governments, including those of Britain and West Germany, to intervene in
youth labour markets in order to offset a catastrophic failure of the 'natural'
level of demand. They have done so partly by removing support for youth
wage rates, arguing that unemployment was due to young workers pricing
themselves out of jobs. But by itself this measure is relatively slow working
and, in the event, unpredictable in its consequences (for example, Dombois,
1989). More rapid action against youth joblessness was achieved by setting
up what colleagues and I have elsewhere conceptualized as 'surrogate' youth
labour markets. In a surrogate labour market unemployed workers are
released to employers under non-contractual arrangements for limited spells
of so-called work experience or skills training. The state administers,
monitors and (usually) subsidizes these programmes in varying degrees and
we argue that the outcome in each case can be explained by the precise mix of
administrative intervention and subsidy, as against unregulated commercial
forces, used in particular schemes (Lee et al., 1990).

In the FRG, as we have seen, the mechanisms for a highly administered
surrogate labour market already existed through the non-standard contracts
of the legally regulated apprenticeship system which imposes a social
obligation on employers to undertake costly skilled training. Even so, the
recession of the early eighties brought criticism of the system to a head
because it seemed possible that the supply of apprenticeship places would fall.

Fearing more direct state intervention, however, the existing mechanisms enabled West German employers to override short-run commercial considerations relatively easily and the number of apprenticeships was maintained; a development from which the whole economy has subsequently benefited (Casey, 1986; Streeck *et al.*, 1987).

In Britain by contrast an expansion of surrogate employment occurred but largely in line with the commercial self interest of individual firms. The powers of the administrative authorities were weak from the outset and have subsequently declined. The result has been worsening skill shortages and the re-emergence of poor work in the guise of youth training.

From the mid seventies, in fact, it was increasingly clear that the youth of the country was returning to the situation that had existed in the earlier years of the century (Roberts, 1984). As youth unemployment climbed to a post-war high, voluntary training provision in industry collapsed dramatically. It was left to the Government to respond to the situation. It did so by means of a rapid expansion of state training programmes in which the common element was the placing of jobless school leavers, as well as other unemployed, onto employers' premises without regular employment contracts, for periods of subsidized work experience and training. However it was argued, particularly within the trade union movement, that these schemes simply revived the unpopular and temporary youth instruction centres of the inter-war slump, which had themselves dressed up job creation and social control of the young unemployed and devalued the idea of training in the process (Rees and Rees, 1982). To this old fear has been added the more contemporary one of workfare. 'Workfare' is an American term applied to a diversity of schemes in individual states in which claimants receive social security benefits in return for work (Burghes, 1987). Critics of the Thatcher Governments of the eighties claim that the latest training schemes mean the introduction of the workfare principle by stealth.

In fact, it was the Labour Government who introduced the Youth Opportunities Programme (YOP) for the young unemployed in 1975. Managed by the newly set up Manpower Services Commission (MSC) it offered jobless school leavers six months of work experience. But YOP was rapidly expanded in the early eighties as youth unemployment soared and, in its expanded form, YOP became rapidly discredited. Unambiguous evidence emerged that employers 'sponsoring' trainees, many of them very small firms, were using the scheme as cheap labour (Finn, 1987). A growing proportion of YOP graduates simply fell back into unemployment. By 1982 the pressures from the MSC and the public to introduce a better quality alternative were irresistible.

What emerged was the Youth Training Scheme (YTS) whose structure resulted from the deliberations of the Youth Task Group, a specially established body which included employer and trade union representatives. It was introduced, however, only after considerable negotiations between the Group and the Government over the Employment minister's desire to discontinue benefit for young unemployed who refused the training. The result was a compromise between the Government's need to get young people out of the unemployment statistics, the free market rhetoric of its overall strategy, the more interventionist philosophy of the trade unions and some MSC staff, and finally the reluctance of employers to see any encroachment on their right to manage.

The structure of YTS has been constantly modified to meet the stream of criticism aimed at it from the outset. As it has changed it has given the appearance of moving British industrial training closer to German practice (Marsden and Ryan, 1989b). YTS initially offered jobless young people a whole year of *planned* work experience and training on an employer's premises and in 1986 the one year was extended to two. Furthermore, it was envisaged that YTS would gradually absorb and replace existing apprentice-ships and traineeships for young people who were already in employment. The stated aim was to develop a national programme of both foundation and occupational training, leading to recognized credentials. While receiving this training and work experience trainees are paid a government training allowance which is half the average for regular youth employment. The subsidy element has encouraged employers to provide placements and schemes of training. It includes grants which cover part of training costs. It represents a state commitment to training which 'in terms of funding and longevity, far exceeds that to any of the transient multitude of other (i.e. earlier) training measures' (ibid, p. 13). Furthermore, minimum quality standards are laid down and supervised by the Government's Training Agency (TA) (formerly the Manpower Services Commission) and linked to an emerging system of National Vocational Qualifications. Recently, in a possible further gesture toward West German institutions, the running of YTS and all other Government training measures has been devolved onto local employer Councils known as Technical and Enterprise Councils (or TECs).

Despite these features, YTS remains heavily dependent on employer voluntarism and it has not seriously challenged 'managements' right to manage' workplace relations, training and youth labour. It preserves voluntarism primarily because the basic availability of places and training depends on a large number of individual initiatives from employers and commercial training organizations who 'offer' to take trainees on the basis of encouragement from the MSC/TA and exhortation from the Government. Indeed, the policy documents which announced the establishment of YTS continued to insist that 'training is industry's responsibility' and not that of the state. Furthermore, the scheme has been surrounded with a rhetoric of neo-liberal ideology which depicts it as 'returning' training to employers and market forces after the 'socialistic' era of the Industry Training Boards (which have now been wound up). 'Management rights' at the grassroots were never even in doubt because employer representatives on the Task Group insisted, as a condition of their voluntary co-operation with YTS, that workplace (on-the-job) training should not be externally monitored, supervised or assessed. It was to be 'blackboxed', that is regulated only by certain somewhat vaguely specified lists of so-called 'competence objectives' which employers themselves voluntarily monitored (Keep, 1986).

Over time glaring defects have emerged in the working of YTS which can be directly attributed to this persistence of voluntarism and absolute management rights over training. First, although there was a rhetoric of altruism in the early days of the schemes it is now clear that the pattern of 'volunteering' has been shaped by the impact of the level of subsidy on the commercial interests of the individual firms concerned. Despite its overall size in relation to past state expenditures on training, much of the funding has been absorbed in creating special public sector places in areas of high unemployment. The remainder still available for more prosperous sectors of the economy has not been adequate to induce large high skill firms to expand costly training in transferable skills. On the other hand it has given a direct labour subsidy to employers in various low skill industries, mostly in the service sector. The result has been a voluntary pattern of provision which, on the available evidence, is not really addressed to the skill shortages in the economy but is training too many youngsters in skills 'not in short supply' (Deakin and Pratten, 1987; Ashton, Maguire and Spilsbury, 1990).

Worse, because trainees are not on a regular employment contract and their work situation is not externally monitored, there are clear signs that in some firms and industries they have become part of a wider trend toward 'flexibility' in employment practices as firms attempt to cope with the insecure trading conditions of the eighties (Pollert, 1987; Lee, 1989; Ashton, Maguire and Spilsbury, 1990). Little appears to have been achieved either in mitigating gender and racial divisions in youth training (Cockburn, 1987; Finn, 1987). So as with YOP, the use of so-called 'trainees' to do the poor work traditionally done by young people has continued.

At the same time the low level of external control has meant the survival of poor training as well as poor work. The supervisory staff of the MSC/TA were given powers to approve YTS schemes for grants but little authority to enforce planned training proposals or independently assess what the young people had learned during their training. The quality of YTS instruction in firms has tended, like apprenticeships in the past to be too beholden to the views of line management and too restricted in content and scope by production pressures and deadlines. This problem has arguably become worse as the Government has actually reduced the powers of the Training Agency. It has also gradually cut the subsidy element especially with the introduction of a second year of training in 1986. Because employers now make a payment for having a YTS trainee they are able to insist on being allowed the discretion to use what they have paid for as they think fit. Even worse, the general employment level has revived at the same time so that it is now in the interests of many firms to offer young people ordinary jobs again rather than YTS. Outside craft occupations, where YTS absorbed old apprenticeship, the number of places has tended to decline, leaving the more prosperous parts of the country with a serious viability problem.

The latest developments in national policy have actually reinforced 'management rights' and the blackboxing of training. In setting out guidelines for a national system of vocational credentials, the responsible body, the National Council for Vocational Qualifications, has opted for 'employer based assessment' a heavily criticized decision (Jarvis and Prais, 1988) which will leave individual employers largely to validate their own training. Furthermore the Training and Enterprise Councils do not have the same statutory authority over all employers of the West German Chambers of Trade. In effect, a privatization of the whole national training system is envisaged which will pass control of schemes like YTS to *ad hoc* consortia of local employers.

CONCLUSION

How badly young people actually suffer from their vulnerability to low paid, poor quality employment depends on a range of institutional factors and national differences in culture and politics. Neither of the societies we examined has been wholly successful in regulating what happens to young people in the workplace. In the FRG, however, law, politics and industrial relations seek to put employers' commercial operations within a framework of social obligations. These include the observance of externally controlled standards of apprentice training which go some way to equipping young people with long-term skills and limiting the number who end up in poor work.

In Britain, the legacy of *laissez-faire* 'free market' politics has placed no such restrictions on employers 'right to manage' youth labour. Consequently, the British economy continues to lack an adequately skilled labour force. For education and training belong to a range of so-called 'public goods' on which commercial success depends but which the market by itself cannot provide (Streeck, 1989). Similarly, recent attempts to 'cure' youth unemployment by forcing youth wages down further, or by creating a cheap 'surrogate' labour force of trainees, have resulted in more poor jobs, making it even 'more attractive to profit making firms to work young people hard rather than to train them'. Only a national system of regulated and obligatory workplace training can overcome these market pressures (Marsden and Ryan, 1988). Indeed, the obligation to give young workers skills and training rather than poor work should in any case need no justification.

7

Recession, redundancy and age

C. C. HARRIS

INTRODUCTION

The disadvantaged character of the elderly has been a matter of concern in Britain and other capitalist societies for over a hundred years. The classic investigations of poverty by Booth (1894) and Rowntree (1901) at the turn of the century established beyond all doubt that the prime causes of poverty were low wages, unemployment and inability to work due to sickness and old age. It was the recognition of the importance of age as a cause of poverty that led to the introduction of old age pensions in 1908, and with it the concept of retirement. Central to these provisions was the notion of payment of pension on the cessation of work.

The coming of pensionable retirement served to constitute the old as a social category which had a negative image. In industrial societies full membership of the society is accorded on the basis of participation in industrial activity rather than as a result of family or community status: it is achieved rather than ascribed. Such societies are dominated by a 'work ethic' which prescribes work as a social duty and makes the significance of life depend on paid work rather than the other way round. As a result those who are not in employment are regarded as at best peripheral and unimportant members of society and their loss of full membership in the moral sense is powerfully reinforced by the loss of purchasing power which results from the reduction of income on retirement from full-time employment.

In the late 1970s and 1980s the labour force was growing. In 1977 the Government introduced the Job Release Scheme designed to encourage older workers to leave their jobs before statutory retirement age. During the 1980s, in the face of a falling or low demand for labour induced by the world recession and government attempts to squeeze inflation out of the system, the policy of labour force reduction was extended by youth training measures. In

1987 youth entry to the labour force began to fall as a result of a previous sharp decline in the birth rate, and by 1989, the persistence of substantial rates of unemployment not withstanding, considerable anxiety was being expressed about the future supply of labour.

With the establishment of the Welfare State after World War Two the link between retirement and eligibility for a pension took the form of an earnings rule whereby pensioners were limited in the amount they were permitted to earn. This rule has been progressively relaxed, most recently in the autumn of 1989. It is evident therefore that whether older people can and ought to continue working and for how long is not a matter which is determined primarily by judgements about *them* and their capacities but rather reflect perceptions about labour supply.

Like women, older age groups have always constituted a 'reserve army' of labour (Phillipson, 1978; Graebner, 1980), encouraged to leave the labour force in times of labour abundance and remain in it at times of labour shortage (Walker, 1983). So we find the Introduction to a Nuffield funded study of 'Ageing in Industry' (Le Gros Clark and Dunne, 1955) remarking that:

A necessary assumption in the present enquiry is that a high demand for labour will persist, and that employers will show a steadily increasing appreciation of the capabilities of the ageing (p. x)

an assumption which explains the purpose of the study:

to determine, so far as we can, what numbers of workers are physically able to continue in their various occupations beyond their mid sixties.

In contrast, during the period between 1970 and 1987, in Britain and other Western European countries, policy has been directed towards motivating older people to withdraw from paid employment at increasingly early ages, and not, as in the 1950s and 1960s, maintaining activity beyond pensionable age. This has led to a dramatic fall in the activity rates of older (55–65 year old) workers. If however a shortage of new labour market entrants results in the demand for labour exceeding supply, we may well, in the 1990s, see a return to the policies of the immediate post-war period.

It is necessary to begin this chapter in such a manner in order to make it clear that there is, in material reality, no naturally defined category of people who are economically disadvantaged by virtue of their age. On the one hand the existence of a statutory retirement age necessarily entails a reduction of income; the 'pensioner' category is socially constructed. On the other hand, there is the progressive loss of working capacity over the latter part of the life course. This does not however generate an age category but is a by-product of the physiological ageing process. This loss of capacity varies markedly between individuals and interacts with their labour market 'position', that is, their chances of obtaining different types of work. Hence loss of capacity affects different types of workers at different ages, forcing some to relinquish their life-time occupation well before reaching retirement age but enabling others to continue to work after it; enabling some to continue in other forms of economic activity after the loss of their life-time occupation and preventing others from any form of economic participation.

However, loss of life-time occupation is not determined uniquely by loss of capacity; nor is continued activity after that loss determined uniquely by residual capacity. Both are determined by the importance accorded by employers to age category membership as a criterion for hiring, firing and transfer between jobs and their willingness to organize work in such a way that tasks are defined which older workers, having reduced capacity, can perform. Different employer policies can have markedly different effects on the ability of workers to continue in employment as Lyon (1985) has shown.

These are generalities. Their importance depends not merely on the extent of employer beliefs concerning age-related disabilities but also on the extent to which employers have occasion to exercise them, and this, in turn, depends on the character of the labour market. If the market is both tight and stable, employers will be hanging on to what labour they have and be unable to recruit more. Hence both actual and perceived age-related disability will not be an important determinant of the employment of older workers because there will be few occasions on which age can be used as a criterion when *engaging* (taking on) workers or *discharging* (sacking) them.

This chapter is entitled 'Recession, Redundancy and Age' because recession provokes labour shedding. There is therefore an opportunity for employers to discriminate against older workers when shedding labour, thus creating a pool of older workers seeking work against whom discrimination may be then exercised again when labour comes once more to be taken on. At the same time a surplus of labour removes all incentive for employers to organize work so that older workers are enabled to continue to participate.

The title includes 'recession' for another reason however. Older workers who lose their jobs at the commencement of a long period of recession become long-term unemployed during which time they become even older and often lose more capacity. By the time the market reaches a point that employers are so desperate for labour that their need overrides their prejudice against both older workers and the long-term unemployed, such workers may well have reached their sixties, and neither they nor employers will see much point in their taking new employment; hence the conjunction of age-related redundancy. The commencement of the recession created a group of people who will be entering that period of economic disadvantage known as old age, after a period of economic disadvantage associated with prolonged unemployment. Their position will deteriorate even further as the value of the old age pension is eroded to encourage younger and more fortunate people to be 'responsible' and make their own private provision for old age.

The rest of this chapter examines the relation of age to economic activity, unemployment and redundancy and discusses the consequences of what is euphemistically termed 'early retirement' with reference to Britain in the 1980s and early 1990s.

AGE, ECONOMIC ACTIVITY AND UNEMPLOYMENT

Economic activity

During the period 1971 to 1991 the population of working age (16 to statutory retirement) has been increasing, the projected figure for 1991 being greater than that for 1971 by 2.6 million, an increase of 8.6 per cent. The civilian labour force, that is, that part of the population over 16 years of age which is economically active actually fell between 1981 and 1983 but has resumed its growth thereafter and is projected to show a net rise over the period of 2.3 million, or 9.2 per cent. This growth is partly the effect of the increase in the population of working age and partly the effect of changes in activity rates. Women's economic activity has increased throughout the period except in the years 1982 and 1983. Men's economic activity has declined throughout the period, falling substantially during the seventies and very markedly during the years 1982 and 1983. Labour force growth has occurred because increases in women's activity have been slightly greater than the falls in men's activity so that there has been a small growth due to increased total economic activity in addition to growth from population change.

The economically active are defined as those *working or seeking* work. Changes in the number of those active do not therefore include changes in the number of the unemployed. Changes in aggregate activity rates are due to changes in age of entry by the 'young' and in age of departure by the 'old'. They are also due to changes in the numbers of 'discouraged workers', that is, those of working age, without employment who are not actively seeking employment, though they would nevertheless like to have a job. The Labour Force Survey describes these workers as believing that there were no jobs available. This is misleading. The point is that they believe there are no jobs obtainable by people in *their* labour market *position*. For example, a 64-year old will not seek work because he knows that no employer will take on an employee for one year (that is, until statutory retirement).

Activity rates are therefore affected by employment levels, since these are related to the balance of supply and demand for labour. The greater the excess of supply over demand, the more discriminating employers will be in recruitment, choosing prime age workers (25–44 years) rather than the inexperienced and untrained young or the allegedly out-of-date and decrepit old, and hence the greater degree of discouragement in disfavoured categories.

An examination of economic activity rates for different age groups illustrates the age related effects of the recession and the economic restructuring that has succeeded it. Activity rates for prime male workers fell by only 1.4 per cent to 94 per cent since 1971, and the rate for 20–24-year old males fell by 3.7 per cent to 84 per cent. In marked contrast the rates for the 45–59 and 60–64-year old males fell by 6.8 and 32.1 per cent to 87.9 and 50.8 per cent, respectively. The rate for the male 65+ age group fell by 13.6 per cent to 5.6 per cent. Activity rates for women under 60 have risen over the period; the rises being greatest among prime age women (16 per cent), followed by those aged 20–24 and 45–54 (9 and 9.8 per cent) and least among women aged 50–59 (0.89 per cent). Activity rates of women over 60 fell sharply by 8.6 per cent to only 5.6 per cent. Changes in economic activity are therefore strongly age related, and falls in male economic activity have been greatest and rises in female activity smallest among the older age groups.

The official explanation of declining activity among older men is that it is due to 'early retirement'. Laczko (1987) has however argued that discouragement lowers the numbers of older workers counted as unemployed by shifting them from the economically active to the inactive and that estimates of discouragement based on the Labour Force Survey underestimate market-induced inactivity because of the tendency for discouraged older workers to re-define themselves as retired or sick. He also shows by comparing the age distributions of the work-force and 'discouraged' workers that the latter (even when narrowly defined) are strongly over-represented in older age groups. 'Discouragement' is related both to labour market conditions and to age. Similar considerations apply to women, except that they describe themselves as housewives rather than retired or sick. It therefore appears that discouragement, widely defined, plays a major part in reducing the official activity rates among the old and that in consequence unemployment rates among the older age groups do not accurately reflect the number of older people who have been deprived of the opportunity to work by market conditions.

Unemployment

Unemployment in Britain rose from 751 000 in 1971 to 2.9 million in 1982. In spite of changes in the unemployment count designed to reduce the numbers of officially unemployed (no less than 24 changes have been introduced which have had this effect) the officially unemployed rose to 3.2 million in July 1986. The Unemployment Unit Index (UUI), which adjusts figures to take account of changes in the unemployment count, estimates the July 1986 figure at 3.6 million. Since then unemployment has declined steadily, the official count falling to 1.8 million and the UUI to 2.3 million by June 1989. In June 1986 the Government introduced changes in the way the unemployment rate was calculated. Thereafter the official rate and the UUI rate diverge slightly (by about 1.4 per cent) quite apart from differences in count. In percentage terms official unemployment rose from 3 per cent in

1971 to 11.7 per cent by July 1986, and fell to 6.2 per cent by July 1989. The UUI rates are 3, 13.5 and 8.2 per cent respectively.

The chief cause of unemployment is changes in the number of jobs available relative to the economically active labour force. Instead of the number of jobs increasing to absorb the increase in the economically active population, they actually decreased by 545 000 between 1971 and 1986, the sharpest fall occurring between December 1979 and March 1983 when, 1 969 000 jobs were lost. Between March 1983 and June 1988 1 208 000 jobs have been created.

Engagements fell sharply after June 1980 and dropped substantially below the rate of discharge which increased. Discharges fell during 1981 and have remained constant since then. Engagements only overtook discharges in 1987. The slow and lagged fall in unemployment, after recession bottomed out in the years 1982 – 1983, is due to the rate of discharge remaining substantial and to engagements rising only slowly. There has therefore been ample opportunity for age discrimination to make itself felt both in firing and hiring. The first implies that the old will constitute a larger proportion of the unemployed and have higher unemployment rates; the second that they will be over-represented among the longer-term unemployed. In more colloquial terms they will be more likely to lose their jobs and be less likely to be taken back on when the market improves. Hence it is to be expected that the relative position of the old will actually deteriorate as the market picks up.

The proportion of 'long-term' male unemployed (over 12 months) in all male unemployed has increased steadily from 22.4 per cent in 1981 to 45.8 per cent in 1987. 1988 showed a slight fall for the first time. The same proportion formed by the very long-term male unemployed (over 3 years) has risen from 8.5 per cent in 1983 to 22.5 per cent in 1988. For women, long-term unemployment has risen from 15.5 to 30.7 per cent and very long-term unemployment from 4.2 to 12.4 per cent over the same period. The continuing growth of long-term unemployment in spite of substantial falls in the unemployment rate indicates how difficult it is to get back into work after long periods of unemployment.

Since 1984 the proportion formed by the older male workers (45+) of the long-term unemployed has increased from 31.9 per cent in 1984 to 38.5 per cent in 1988, whereas the proportion formed by men under 25 has decreased from 25.2 to 16 per cent, and this in spite of changes in the unemployment count consequent upon the 1983 budget which reduced the number of male claimants over 60 years by an estimated 162 000 of whom 125 000 were long-term unemployed. The proportion of the long-term unemployed formed by women over 45 years has increased even more sharply – from 31.6 per cent in 1984 to 42.5 per cent in 1988, while the proportion formed by women under 25 has fallen from 41 to 25.8 per cent. These figures confirm that the position of older workers is in fact deteriorating as market conditions improve.

If we examine unemployment rates the same picture of disadvantage and relative deterioration of position among older workers emerges. In both July 1986 and July 1989 unemployment was highest among men who were under 25 years and aged 50–59 years. While unemployment levels had been reduced by between one-third and two-fifths in the younger age groups, they had fallen by only one-fifth in the 50–59 year category. Among women aged 50–59 years, unemployment levels had fallen by two-fifths but among younger women the fall was between one-half and two-thirds.

Once an older worker becomes unemployed he or she is less likely to be re-employed because they are old. Being less likely to be re-employed means that they will remain a longer time unemployed. Being long-term unemployed further reduces their chance of re-employment. The data substantiate this argument in spite of the fact that they underestimate the disadvantage older people experience. Being unable to find work they will stop looking and hence become 'discouraged workers', or redefine themselves as 'sick' or 'retired' and hence not be classified as active. If these workers were included in the statistics cited above the degree of disadvantage of the older workers would be shown to be even greater.

THE ROLE OF REDUNDANCY

Workers' age disadvantages them in their search for employment even when market conditions are improving. All age categories increased their chances of ceasing to be unemployed between 1984 and 1987, but once again the older categories improved their chances much less than the younger categories. But are older workers more likely to lose their employment? Here the situation is more complicated. Younger people change jobs more frequently than older people and job changing frequently involves a spell of unemployment. Hence older people are less likely to *become* unemployed as well as less likely to *cease* to be unemployed than younger people.

Because older people are less likely to become unemployed through leaving their jobs, it does not follow that they do not become unemployed through *losing* their jobs. If older people do have a greater likelihood of being discharged than younger people this should be reflected in the unemployment rates for 1981 when the discharge rate was at its highest. In fact, in that year, the level of unemployment among 50–59-year-old men increased by a proportion greater than any other age group over 20 years, and this in spite of the fact that a proportion of those in this group who lost their jobs would have been classified as retired. The changes in levels for women show little variation with age. With regard to older men, we can conclude that they have not only a greater propensity to *remain* unemployed but also to *become* unemployed than do younger age groups, in spite of the fact that generally older workers are less likely to leave their jobs.

The reason that older workers are more likely to become unemployed is due to the use by employers of statutory redundancy to discharge workers.

The reason that this increases older workers' chances of being discharged is linked with the statutory provision connected with redundancy. This was designed to facilitate the *redeployment* of workers in an era of full employment. It provided for redundancy payments which were positively related to length of service and the Redundancy Fund, established by the 1965 Redundancy Act, paid a greater proportion of the cost of redundancy to employers in respect of workers over the age of 41. As a result, acceptance of redundancy became more attractive to older workers. As early as 1974, the British Institute of Management was able to conclude that age was the most important criterion for redundancy selection (Employment Gazette, 1978; Jolly, 1980). However, as unemployment rose during the 1970s the effect of the redundancy legislation ceased to be to encourage workers to adapt to structural change in the economy. The lump sums were no longer used to pay removal expenses and learn new skills but provided instead an inducement to withdraw from employment. *Redeployment* redundancy had become (hidden) *unemployment* redundancy for those within less than ten years of retirement.

In the late 1960s and 1970s redundancy was not a form of net job loss however. Jobs were, of course, lost through redundancy but they were replaced by new jobs elsewhere. In the 1980s this changed as the total number of jobs fell. Jobs lost were not replaced and redundancy became one of the ways in which employment declined. Jobs can disappear through natural wastage or through redundancy. Natural wastage involves not replacing employees when they leave. The majority of job disappearances in the 1970s were the result of wastage, not of redundancy: the redundancy curve remained fairly flat, though showing a tendency to rise. After July 1979, all the redundancy measures started to rise (Noble, 1981). By 1980, confirmed redundancies were at 2.8 times the 1978 levels and peaked at 532 000 or three times the 1978 level in 1981. Thereafter redundancies fell until by 1984 they had reached their pre-recession level. In manufacturing alone, over one million jobs disappeared through redundancy in the recession years 1980 – 1982.

The significance of the increasing importance of redundancy as a type of job loss during the recession is that it affects the age distribution of any unemployment that it generates. Natural wastage involves not replacing workers who leave. If workers who leave are replaced they are not necessarily replaced with workers of the same age as those who have left. The general tendency is to replace older workers lost through ill health or retirement by recruitment of young people, while the age pattern of replacement of losses of workers at ages other than those of retirement is determined by the age composition of job seekers rather than that of job leavers. Hence natural wastage, that is, not replacing workers, on balance tends to reduce the labour market chances of younger age groups relative to those who are older and hence increase youth unemployment.

Redundancy, whether compulsory or voluntary, tends to push older workers into unemployment and *out of the labour market.* The rise in the level of redundancies between 1979 and 1984, that is the increased use of redundancy as a method of labour force reduction, has tended to shift disadvantage away from the younger age group and towards older workers. At the depth of the recession of course both tendencies were manifest at the same time: employers continued not to recruit young labour market entrants and reduced their established work-force by redundancy, thus pushing predominantly older workers onto or out of the market.

It will be seen therefore that a greater tendency for older workers to lose their jobs tends to be associated with recession as a process. It is not associated with levels of unemployment, high or low, but with periods of rapid job loss which are in turn associated with periods of recession. Older workers, like other disadvantaged groups in the market, become even more disadvantaged in the search for employment when markets are loose, and unemployment is high. But provided that situation has been reached by job loss through natural wastage and not redundancy they will not necessarily be forced to search for employment and will not therefore experience high rates of unemployment.

It could be argued that as older workers move in and out of employment less than younger workers, the sudden increase in the older unemployed experienced in the recession years is a 'recession' phenomenon which will not persist and will only affect the labour market experience of those workers who happened to be in the last twenty years of their working life when recession struck. This argument is valid as far as it goes; that is to say the old and the young have borne a disproportionate burden of the costs of recession, and new cohorts will not be required to bear the same cost. However if the argument were wholly correct then we should expect older workers' share of unemployment to fall as the cohort affected by the recession moves into retirement and their numbers are not replaced because of the fall in the level of redundancies. In fact their share of unemployment at July 1989 was rather higher than it was in July 1987. There is therefore some doubt that the disadvantage experienced by older workers during the recent recession is a transitory phenomenon. The reasons for this are the unsatisfactory nature of the available statistics and conceptual and methodological confusion over the notion of retirement (see Parker, 1982, p. 31ff).

The problem of retirement

By retirement most people understand permanent withdrawal from economic activity on receipt of a pension, and early retirement to be retirement at an age earlier than that society expected or statutorily prescribed. It follows that early retirement should also involve withdrawal and receipt of alternative income. The most frequent source of alternative income before statutory retirement age is a pension from an occupational pension scheme. However, unlike the original statutory pensions scheme, occupational pensions are not conditional on withdrawal from economic activity but only upon withdrawal from engagement in the life-time activity in the employment of the worker's previous employer. Hence it is possible to add to an occupational pension by taking further employment after 'retirement'. Conversely, for those outside occupational pensions schemes, withdrawal from economic activity on the grounds of ill health, or as a result of job loss plus 'discouragement', or both, frequently occurs in spite of the fact that no alternative, 'as of right' income is available, subsistence being provided by supplementary or sickness benefit. The introduction by the Government in 1986 of a scheme whereby men over 60-years old were eligible for a higher rate of supplementary benefit on condition that they became economically inactive is merely an official response to what was occurring spontaneously and contrasts with the Job Release Scheme which, as we have seen, was designed in 1977 to encourage withdrawal from employment. Moreover successive relaxation of the earnings rule further weakens the link between 'retirement' and withdrawal.

Now if there is 'retirement' without pension and pension eligibility without any condition of withdrawal, this necessarily affects the permanence of withdrawal at the point of retirement. Participants in generous occupational schemes may be able to afford to abandon their life-time activity before either the statutory retirement age or their declining abilities necessitates. In which case they, may after a time, resume some form of remunerated activity. Some of those forced out of occupation through ill health will return to work to increase their income if suitable work can be found. Those who classify themselves as retired but who are really discouraged workers will return to economic activity for the same reason as soon as market conditions permit.

Now whether we call cessation of employment before the statutory retirement age 'early retirement' or whether we refer instead to the low economic activity rates of older workers, the impression given is that of voluntary withdrawal made possible by increasing affluence and an enhanced capacity for the use of leisure. Indeed studies of early retirees have tended to reinforce this impression. Studies conducted in the sixties emphasized the high degree of satisfaction of early retirees with life after retirement. However as Parker (1982) has pointed out many of these surveys were studies of special groups, rather than representative samples and his own study (Parker, 1980) found that 44 per cent regretted early retirement.

Although it is impossible to quantify, the available evidence suggests that much voluntary retirement in the 1980s was voluntary only in name [see, for example, Bytheway (1985) and Cliff (1989)]. Workers are frequently asked to volunteer for redundancy under threat of compulsory redundancy if not enough volunteers come forward. Atkinson (1985) quotes a personnel manager as saying:

> You must understand that we don't just announce the scheme and then sit back and wait. You could almost describe our scheme as a compulsory voluntary early retirement scheme. (p. 28)

and one of Cliff's (1989) respondents remarked:

> It was the company's decision at the end of the day. There was no way I
> could avoid it. If I hadn't gone they would have found a way of easing
> me out . . . (p. 7)

The workers at BSC Port Talbot in Bytheway's study were encouraged to take
redundancy 'to save steel making at Port Talbot' and in this instance there
was the pressure, widely reported from other studies of redundancy during
the recession, of moral persuasion being used: it is the duty of older
employees to go to make jobs available for younger workers.

If severance only has the appearance of voluntariness, so does the decision of unemployed older workers discouraged by failure to obtain employment to reclassify themselves as sick or 'retired'. Those on low wages
are often outside occupational pensions schemes (only half the labour
force is covered by such schemes: Government Actuary, 1986) or eligible
only for benefits designed to augment the old age pension. Such workers
cannot afford to retire and their adoption of the retired label is in no sense
voluntary.

Satisfaction among early retirees is directly dependent on the voluntariness of the retirement, which is in turn dependent on the existence of
favourable conditions for early withdrawal. Those alienated by the 'rat
race' or exhausted by physical labour or dogged by ill health will be motivated to consider the possibility of early retirement favourably, while
those who, in addition, have non-work interests which they wish to pursue
and are certain of an adequate post-retirement income are likely to grasp
the opportunity. Hence those on high incomes covered by generous occupational pension schemes and those with low incomes but within two or
three years of retirement are genuinely likely to welcome early withdrawal
and show high rates of satisfaction with their early retirement experience.
The converse is true of those forced into 'voluntary' early retirement either
by the exigencies of production or the operation of the market (Walker,
1985).

It is clear therefore that there are two nations in early retirement just as
there are two nations in old age. Between 1951 and 1971 retirement appears to be related to the use by both employers and unions of statutory
pension provision to manage exit from the labour force. Early retirement
in contrast was chosen by economically privileged workers in occupational
pensions schemes. By 1981, however, early retirement becomes significantly related to mortality. These results, from a statistical study by
Johnson (1988), are interpreted by the author as the result of employers
using ill health as a criterion for compulsory redundancy. This ignores
however the attractiveness of nominally voluntary redundancy to older
workers and begs the question of the relation between ill health, mortality
and redundancy. It does indicate however an emergence, even by 1981, of
two nations in early retirement as well as in retirement itself.

AGE AND STRATIFICATION

It is clear from the available evidence that advanced age is not in itself a characteristic which assigns those of older ages to a necessarily inferior economic position. In the first place many older non-manual workers reach the peak of their earning capacity later in life at a point in their life course when their outgoings on accommodation and children are at their lowest. This makes possible substantial savings and investment income from savings which together with generous pension provision can make retirement for the 'new old' as they have been called, if not a period of relative prosperity, then at least a period not marked by relative deprivation in economic terms.

When we turn to the working class, it is not the case that age itself is a characteristic which operates to create polarization: there is no simple subdivision of the impoverished old and the affluent young. Older employees in employment are not subject to disadvantage relative to younger working-class people in employment, and later working life even in the working class is unlikely to be a period of deprivation relative to early stages in the life course. It is the retirement period itself when deprivation is felt most severely since pension provisions are poor and income levels while working do not make possible capital accumulation on a significant scale. If we restrict our attention to those in employment, then, later life is a period in which people experience loss of working capacity and the income consequences of this loss are felt most severely by the working class.

In contrast age becomes of considerable importance as a factor in creating disadvantage as soon as we move from the place of employment to the labour market. Here, as we have seen, the older worker, once on the market, is less likely to be re-employed and more likely to experience long-term unemployment. Age does not necessarily disadvantage all those older workers 'in' the market, that is, all the economically active. It does disadvantage those 'on' the market. It does not follow however that age is one aspect of a market segment. Older workers are not concentrated in particular types of jobs in the way that women and blacks frequently are. Unless they are, we cannot talk of older workers constituting a market segment as opposed to a segment of job applicants. Reduction in working capacity is a natural phenomenon and through the social category 'older worker' the market amplifies the economic consequence of this natural disadvantage during those periods and in those places and in those occupations where an abundance of labour makes selective recruitment possible.

This chapter has been concerned however with the connection between employment and the market. Changes in production (in response to changes in product markets) can and have during the eighties generated redundancies. Existing redundancy schemes are financially attractive to older workers and motivate employers to make older workers redundant. Therefore, older workers in employment though not disadvantaged while in employment are more likely to lose employment through redundancy, and go onto the market where they are less likely to obtain employment. They have, during the eighties, therefore had a greater tendency both to fall into and remain in the disadvantaged stratum of the working class.

We have considered the inconclusive evidence concerning whether, in future tighter labour markets with lower rates of redundancy, older workers will continue to be disadvantaged in these ways. An answer to this question requires consideration of the grounds of employers' prejudice against older workers. There are, as it happens, several grounds for the belief that older workers are less desirable employees. First, in the past, when much labour was heavy and arduous, older workers experienced occupationally-induced ill health which accelerated the decline of physical efficiency associated with age. The second ground is associated not with physiological decline but with the duration of working life. Members of the labour force are educated to levels thought appropriate at the time of their youth, a quarter of a century before they enter the 'older' category. Given rapid and accelerating technological advance, these levels are likely to be below those required 25 years later. The third ground is distinct but associated with the second. Types of skill or skill content change with technological innovation and the volume of training or retraining required to attain the required level increases with technological advance. Grounds two and three then interact. 'Low' educational levels make retraining for higher skills more costly.

This may be put another way. The value of the 'work capital' embodied in the worker declines with time (rather than age) and the size of the investment to create the required level of work capital increases and the period during which a return on that capital may be had (the rest of the worker's working life) decreases. In purely economic terms, the older a worker is, the less viable he or she may be as a wage labourer from whom surplus value may be extracted under capitalism (or as a means to the fulfilment of production norms under socialism).

What affects the recruiting and discharge policy of employers is not the reality of older workers' capacities but beliefs about that reality. Because there are valid grounds for supposing that the value of some workers in some occupations declines over time, it is likely that this will inform (and already does inform) a prejudice against (that is, a pre-judgement of) all older workers as a category thus motivating employers to prefer to discharge older workers and not to re-employ them. The danger is that the social construction of the category 'older worker' will amplify the market disadvantage older workers suffer as a consequence of the speed of technological change. Policy should be directed to minimizing this disadvantage, not increasing it by schemes which, under the euphemism of early retirement, amplify economic deprivation in old age by excluding older workers as a category from economic activity in later life.

8
Race, employment and economic change

ROBIN WARD AND MALCOLM CROSS

INTRODUCTION

The phenomenon within world history known as 'race relations' and the associated area of intellectual enquiry and policy intervention bear witness to skin colour having acquired a deep-rooted social meaning which has legitimated the most extreme form of poor work through the institution of slavery and the subsequent concentration of 'racial' minorities within the least privileged and least rewarded sectors of the economy. The history of post-war immigration to the UK from the Caribbean, South Asia and East Africa has been similarly interpreted in terms of discriminatory constraints on the Black and Asian population of migrants and their descendants restricting the chances of employment, and thus perpetuating the reality of 'poor work' within the evolution of the advanced industrial economy.

The aim of this chapter is first, to examine some evidence of the extent to which Blacks and Asians in the UK are disproportionately concentrated in areas of 'poor work', secondly, to set out a broad interpretation of processes of economic change over recent decades which have restructured opportunities for paid work and thirdly to relate this approach to the statistical data on the economic position of racial minorities in Britain. It is concluded that the concentration of ethnic minorities in economically marginal positions in the UK is based on a set of interrelated factors which must be jointly addressed if interventions are to bring the goal of equality in employment significantly closer to reality.

THE ETHNIC MINORITY POPULATION IN THE UK

Immigration to the UK from the Caribbean and South Asia gathered pace during the early post-war years of economic reconstruction, when labour

Table 8.1. Economically active people of working age (16–59/64) by ethnic origin, for regions, 1984–1986 average

Region of residence	White (%)	Non-white (%)	West Indian/ Guyanese (%)	Indian (%)	Pakistani/ Bangladeshi (%)
South East	31.4	57.7	67.1	53.6	35.6
West Midlands	9.2	14.0	14.7	19.0	18.5
East Midlands	7.2	6.4	3.4	12.0	–
North West	11.5	8.1	5.1	7.6	14.1
Yorks and Humberside	8.9	5.7	5.1	3.8	14.1
East Anglia	3.6	1.5	–	–	–
Wales	4.8	1.4	–	–	–
South West	8.2	2.1	–	–	–
Northern	5.6	1.3	–	–	–
Scotland	9.4	1.6	–	–	–
n(000)	25 157	1 035	292	343	135

Source: Department of Employment (1988b, p. 175)

intensive industries were expanding and faced with a chronic labour shortage. The peak years of immigration were those of economic boom, when the demand for labour was at its greatest, in particular during 1960–1962, when the flow of newcomers was increased by the rush of people anticipating the ban on free immigration from the New Commonwealth brought into being by the Commonwealth Immigration Act of 1962 (Rose *et al.*, 1969). The only significant streams of immigrants since then have been the dependants of those already in the UK and Asians with British citizenship from East Africa affected by nativization of the economy, including refugees expelled by President Amin. Over recent years, therefore, growth in the numbers of people with their origins in the Caribbean and South Asia (including those who came from East Africa) has been due to a natural increase within a population with a high proportion of young adults. Indeed, by 1983 two-thirds of those aged under 19 and categorized as 'non-white' were born in the UK (HMSO, 1984).

In the years of unrestricted immigration from the New Commonwealth, Blacks and Asians found employment relatively easy to obtain but were heavily concentrated in low status, badly paid jobs in the traditional manufacturing centres of London, the Midlands, Yorkshire and Lancashire (Rose *et al.*, 1969). Information from the Labour Force Survey for the years 1984–1986 (Department of Employment, 1988b) allows us to see how far this early pattern of high rates of employment in low grades of work in the areas of primary settlement has changed over the years. Table 8.1 summarizes the numbers of people of 'West Indian' and specified Asian origins by place of settlement in the UK.

It is clear from Table 8.1 that the great majority of the economically active ethnic minority population are still concentrated in the regions in which they originally settled. Indeed, the South East and the West Midlands alone account for over 70 per cent [60 per cent within Greater London and the West Midlands County (Department of Employment, 1988b, p. 175)]. A further 20 per cent are located in the other industrial regions of primary settlement: East Midlands, North West and Yorkshire and Humberside. Only 8 per cent are to be found in the remaining regions (East Anglia, Wales, South West, Northern and Scotland) which contain almost one-third of the white economically active population. In the South East and West Midlands the ethnic minority population is substantially over-represented. In the intermediate industrial regions, they are somewhat under-represented. In the regions in the third block they are heavily under-represented.

Table 8.2. Economically active people of working age (16–59/64) by ethnic origin for selected Metropolitan Counties within regions, 1984–1986 average

Metropolitan County/ region of residence	White (%)	Non- white (%)	West Indian/ Guyanese (%)	Indian (%)	Pakistani/ Bangladeshi (%)
South East					
Greater London	48.1	82.4	89.3	81.0	75.0
Rest of South East	51.9	17.6	10.7	19.0	25.0
n(000)	7 909	597	196	184	48
West Midlands					
West Midlands Met. County	47.2	84.8	90.7	84.6	88.0
Rest of West Midlands	52.8	15.2	–	–	–
n(000)	2 322	145	43	65	25
Yorks and Humberside					
South Yorkshire	25.6	16.9	–	–	–
West Yorkshire	41.8	72.9	73.3	92.3	84.2
Rest of Yorks and Humberside	32.6	–	–	–	–
n(000)	2 243	59	15	13	19

Source: Department of Employment (1988b, p. 175)

But how far have the ethnic minority populations dispersed over the regions where they originally settled? Table 8.2 indicates that there is still a heavy concentration in the core areas of these regions. Greater London contains under half of the white population of the South East but over 80 per cent of the Black and Asian population. The over-representation within West Midlands County in the West Midlands is even greater. Broadly similar figures are also found in Yorkshire and Humberside where West Yorkshire County, with less than half of the total population, has retained over 70 per cent of the ethnic minority population in the groups identified.

These figures show the broad picture within the UK. Local surveys convey a similar situation within particular towns and cities (Cross and Johnson, 1988). The significance of these distributions is increased by the fact that the areas of continuing concentration are among those with the highest rate of population decline over the past twenty years.

While there is a clear pattern to the clustering of regions in which ethnic minorities are over- or under-represented, Table 8.3 shows that they are difficult to classify in terms of the *overall* level of unemployment. All three groupings contain regions which have both above average and below average unemployment. However, there are clearer differences in the level of unemployment among the Black and Asian population in the three groups of regions.

Those in which ethnic minorities are over- or somewhat under-represented include all three regions in which almost 30 per cent of the ethnic minority population are out of work. These three regions, West Midlands, North West and Yorkshire and Humberside, have witnessed the greatest decline in manufacturing in recent years, unaccompanied by a compensating rise in service sector employment. Whites in these regions display an unemployment rate about average for the UK. Presumably this has been achieved by a combination of easier access to such jobs as remained and a higher rate of outmigration to other regions with more job opportunities. In all three cases the ethnic minority unemployment rate is two to three times as high as for Whites.

The two other regions within these two groupings are the South East and the East Midlands. The South East has also experienced a high rate of manufacturing decline, but this has been paralleled by a surge in service sector business where alternative jobs have been available. In the East Midlands the manufacturing economy has held up more successfully, and the results of this are shown in below average unemployment for Whites. In both these regions ethnic unemployment is about twice that for Whites.

Finally, the five regions in which ethnic minorities are heavily under-represented include two with the lowest levels of unemployment in the UK and three with the highest. In four of the five cases, however, ethnic minorities have done relatively better, having, with the exception of the South West, unemployment levels substantially lower than twice the corresponding White figure. Indeed in the Northern region there are only two percentage points

Table 8.3. Unemployment rates by ethnic origin for regions, 1984–1986 average, people of working age (16–59/64)

Region of residence	White (%)	Non-white (%)	West Indian/ Guyanese (%)	Indian (%)	Pakistani/ Bangladeshi (%)
South East	8	16	18	11	26
West Midlands	12	29	30	26	40
East Midlands	9	20	24	18	–
North West	13	29	37	26	32
Yorks and Humberside	11	28	31	18	36
East Anglia	8	14	–	–	–
Wales	14	21	–	–	–
South West	8	18	–	–	–
Northern	15	17	–	–	–
Scotland	14	21	–	–	–

Source: Department of Employment (1988b, p. 177)

between the two figures. In the North, Scotland and Wales the bulk of outmigration in search of employment probably preceded the arrival of migrants from the New Commonwealth. Furthermore, the numbers have in all three cases been very small, an indication that there was no demand for jobs in the 1950s and 1960s in large manufacturing sectors that have since lost their competitiveness and contracted sharply. In these regions much of the settlement by Blacks and Asians seems to have been of households rather more widely scattered over local employment. Finally, East Anglia and the South West differ in having had a more stable economy over the longer term, but in both cases the amount of New Commonwealth immigration has been very small.

Table 8.4 breaks down unemployment figures within the South East and the West Midlands. Overall there is little difference between Greater London and the rest of the South East in the level of White and ethnic minority unemployment. But this aggregate figure conceals a substantially higher level of unemployment among those from the Caribbean within Greater London than in the surrounding areas, while among Indians there is a slight reverse tendency.

However, in the West Midlands there is a more dramatic difference between the position in the West Midlands County (roughly synonymous with the Birmingham conurbation) and the less heavily industrialized areas in the surrounding parts of the region. The White unemployment level in the peripheral areas of the region is only two percentage points lower than in the

Table 8.4. Unemployment rates by ethnic origin for Metropolitan Counties within regions, 1984–1986 average, people of working age (16–59/64)

Metropolitan County/ region of residence	White (%)	Non-white (%)	West Indian/ Guyanese (%)	Indian (%)	Pakistani/ Bangladeshi (%)
South East					
Greater London	8	16	19	11	26
Rest of South East	7	14	14	13	25
West Midlands					
West Midlands Met. County	13	32	31	28	46
Rest of West Midlands	11	14	–	–	–

Source: Department of Employment (1988b, p. 177)

County, but for the ethnic minority population, the proportion out of work drops from 32 per cent in the County to 14 per cent outside. This suggests that there has been very limited movement by Blacks and Asians out of the Birmingham area into surrounding districts to avoid unemployment. In contrast, in the light of the sharp decline in the manufacturing sector in the West Midlands over the 1980s, it seems difficult to imagine that the unemployment level among the White population within the County could be kept down to 13 per cent without extensive relocation in search of work.

Finally, Tables 8.3 and 8.4 indicate that there are significant differences in the level of unemployment between minority communities. In all regions, and counties within regions, the lowest unemployment rates are to be found among those classified as Indian, while everywhere except the North West those from Pakistan and Bangladesh have the highest. Those from the Caribbean are in an intermediate position. The fact that the national unemployment rate for Pakistanis and Bangladeshis (31 per cent) is virtually twice as high as for Indians (16 per cent) confirms that the social experience of members of these communities, many of whom were born in the UK, diverges sharply (Department of Employment, 1988, p. 177).

The Labour Force Survey statistics from which Tables 8.3 and 8.4 have been constructed do not permit a systematic comparison of the unemployment levels of men and women by area within the different ethnic minority communities; the numbers of females in many categories were too small to allow figures to be included in the published Tables. Nevertheless, while the piecemeal nature of the available information does not justify presentation in tabular form, some interesting features can be noted.

Within the white population differences in male and female unemployment rates are mostly slight: 1 per cent difference in national figures and no more than 2 or 3 per cent (in favour of women) in particular regions. Nor are the differences in the level of unemployment by gender within regions of any significance. Within the ethnic minority communities the position is quite different. The aggregate unemployment level of 22 per cent for those from the Caribbean can be broken down to 25 per cent among men and 18 per cent among women. Yet within the population of Indian origin there is a slightly higher unemployment rate among the women (18 per cent) compared to men (15 per cent) and among those from Pakistan and Bangladesh a much higher rate for women (38 per cent) compared to men (30 per cent).

Some further insights into this variation can be obtained by examining figures for the South East and the West Midlands, where the numbers involved are relatively large. In the South East, there is no difference in the aggregate unemployment level among ethnic minority men and women, but as suggested above, this conceals a higher unemployment level among men from the Caribbean and among women from India. Further, while Indian male unemployment is about the same in Greater London (9 per cent) and the remainder of the South East (10 per cent), among Indian women there is a large variation: 13 per cent in London compared to 19 per cent in the rest of the South East.

In the West Midlands some of those internal distinctions are present in a more dramatic form. Overall, while White employment rates are virtually identical for men (12 per cent) and women (11 per cent), there is a more marked difference in the aggregate figures for the ethnic minorities: 31 per cent among men and 27 per cent among women. This is a product of large differences within specific minority communities. Thirty-six per cent of male West Indians are unemployed, compared to 23 per cent of females. However, 24 per cent of male Indians are unemployed as against 29 per cent of females. By inference the same pattern can be adduced for those from Pakistan and Bangladesh, though the full figures are not given. Thus, while gender is not a factor which significantly differentiates men and women within the White population in terms of the level of unemployment experienced, there are substantial and conflicting trends to be explained within the minority communities.

A further divergence in the experience of ethnic minorities in the UK is found when we examine the *level* at which people employed. Table 8.5 reveals a complex pattern of ethnic concentration in employment. Among men it is those originating from India who are most likely to be in managerial or professional employment (42 per cent followed by White men with 34 per cent). There is also a slight over-representation of Indian men among those in clerical employment. By contrast, West Indian men are those most likely to be in craft jobs and those from India and Pakistan least likely. Finally the highest levels of employment in other manual jobs are found among those from Pakistan/Bangladesh and the Caribbean. A crude conclusion to be drawn from these figures is that Indian men are somewhat concentrated in higher

Table 8.5. Employment by occupation, ethnic origin and sex, 1984–1986 average, all ages 16 and over

Occupational category	White			Afro-Caribbean			Indian			Pakistani/Bangladeshi			Total		
	M (%)	F (%)	Total (%)	M (%)	F (%)	Total (%)	M (%)	F (%)	Total (%)	M (%)	F (%)	Total (%)	M (%)	F (%)	Total (%)
Managerial and professional	34	25	31	10	27	19	42	25	36	27	35	28	34	25	31
Clerical and non-manual	11	40	23	11	31	21	13	32	19	8	34	12	11	40	23
Craft and similar	26	4	17	34	3	18	20	17	19	17	14	17	26	4	17
Other manual	28	31	29	43	38	41	25	26	25	48	17	43	28	31	29

Source: Department of Employment (1988b, p. 169)

level positions while West Indians and rather more so Pakistanis are concentrated in lower level positions. This shows continuity with the socio-
economic background of the different migrant communities (Rose *et al.*,
1969; Nowikowski, 1984) and suggests that at a broad level, differences in
education, qualifications and employment experience continue to influence
the achievements at work of the following generation.

Among female employees a different pattern emerges. It is those from
Pakistan and Bangladesh who are most likely to be in managerial and professional positions (35 per cent compared to 25–27 per cent for the other
groups). White women are most prominent in clerical level positions.
Asian women are much more likely to be in craft type employment and
West Indian women the most concentrated in other types of manual work.
Overall, the employment experiences of women in the four categories are
much more closely grouped. There is a slight concentration of women
from Pakistan and Bangladesh in higher level positions, but the dominant
feature of the data in Table 8.5 is the irrelevance of ethnic origins to level
of employment for the great majority of women.

While the pattern of ethnic differentiation set out above is complex, the
main distinctions can be summarized in a series of points:

1 *Area of settlement*
   Continuing concentration in industrial regions and in areas of original
   settlement.
2 *Unemployment*
   Substantially higher unemployment for all ethnic minorities than for
   Whites in all regions and areas;
   Substantial inter-ethnic differences: Indians best placed, followed by
   West Indians, the Pakistanis and Bangladeshis.
3 *Level of employment*
   No clear, overall White: ethnic minority differences;
   Indians and Whites more concentrated in higher level positions;
   West Indians and Pakistanis and Bangladeshis in lower level positions.
4 *Gender differences*
   (i)   *Unemployment*: Men better off among Indians, Pakistanis and
         Bangladeshis, women better off among West Indians
   (ii) *Area of settlement*: Indian women worst off in dispersed lo-
         cations, no difference among Whites and West Indians
   (iii) *Level of employment*: Female employment levels more closely
         matched across ethnic minority groups; highest concentration of
         male higher level positions among Indians, of *female* higher level
         positions among Pakistanis and Bangladeshis; no substantial
         gender difference in employment level of Indians/Whites, but
         among West Indians and Pakistanis/Bangladeshis employment
         level of men is substantially lower than among women.

INTERPRETATION

The systematic racial disadvantage which has accompanied ethnic minorities from the New Commonwealth since their arrival in Britain in the 1950s and 1960s is still clearly in evidence (Smith, 1977; Brown, 1984; Brown and Gay, 1985). But the pattern of ethnic differentiation set out above contains features which suggest that the crude tendency to discriminate on racial grounds against those from South Asia and the Caribbean is heavily mediated by features of the socio-economic environment. In looking for an interpretation of the pattern that racial disadvantage now takes, we begin by reviewing some of the main features of global economic change over recent decades in order to identify significant developments in industry structures and in opportunities and demand for paid work.

The large-scale immigration of the 1950s and early 1960s from the Caribbean and South Asia marked the last phase in the increasingly global search for labour by employers in Western economies seeking to maintain their established industrial dominance by economies of scale and traditional, labour-intensive production methods. However, their competitiveness in many global markets was already being undermined by the rise of large firms in the Far East enjoying substantial cost advantages and extending their focus from domestic to international markets. This process has continued as newer forces in global manufacturing, notably Japan, have faced increasing competition in turn from other industrialising economies.

The impact of fierce global competition on Western manufacturing concerns has varied. Some industries, such as motor-cycle manufacturing in Britain, went into terminal decline before any effective way of responding to the new competition could be developed. In some cases, including other sectors of the engineering industry, the main response has been to close down plants in North West Europe and switch investment to low wage economies further afield. A system of global quotas was devised to protect the competitive position of textile firms in Western industrial economies and allow time for restructuring to face changing competitive trends. Increasingly complex joint ventures have been initiated with global competitors designed to buy some of the benefits of their competitive strength.

Underlying many of the adjustments made by Western firms has been a recognition of the changing pattern of demand for their products. At the time of New Commonwealth immigration to Britain there was still a large demand for basic goods and services of a traditional kind sold on price. The philosophy 'pile it high and sell it cheap' was still common currency in many areas of retailing, notably clothing and food. However, this recipe for commercial success was under threat from two sources. First, it was precisely the goods with 'commodity' characteristics which exhibited a stable demand and were sold on price which were most vulnerable to foreign competitors with substantial labour cost advantages. Secondly, the steady growth in disposable income was enabling a long-term trend to become established away from standard products to more differentiated goods and services. Fashion, shown in the more rapid recycling of styles covering an ever wider range of garments, and the development of specialized products for particular uses transformed consumer behaviour. Demand grew, but for products with a distinctive and increasingly international fashionality. Grocery super-market retailing facilitated similar trends in the food industry: less generic goods and more diverse, specialized items sourced increasingly from abroad.

Thus the combined effect of growing international competition and a sharp increase in the differentiation of demand was to question the future competitiveness of many traditional domestic products. Smaller, more flexible firms emerged in response to the growing influence of fashion. Italian design increased its hold on consumers, and retailers reacted by switching orders abroad. Where British design or British capital continued to support manufacturing, it was more and more through off-shore production. All these factors had a serious effect on the competitiveness of British industry and hence on the market position of labour.

Furthermore, the impact of the restructuring of product features and locations of production on the labour force in Britain was matched by the transformation of processes. The most successful industry sectors in the new conditions of international competition tended to be those based on proprietary knowledge (such as pharmaceuticals) or capital intensive prod-uction of highly differentiated goods (such as high quality cars). There was little scope for traditional, labour intensive operations in the new business environment.

The impact of these trends on the labour market position of migrants from the Caribbean and South Asia, together with their children, can easily be appreciated. In some sectors, notably textiles, they had provided the labour force to keep traditional sectors using labour intensive methods competitive, not least by operating the night shift to allow more effective use of capital equipment. But in many instances the economies they provided were insufficient to allow the survival of the business. In other sectors, such as car assembly, the labour force had become more multi-racial but the deterior-ating position of labour led to, often successful, attempts to reclaim jobs for White workers. In particular, the 'lads of dads' could still be offered prior access to jobs on the grounds of family connections in the firm and local residence (Lee and Wrench, 1983).

This transformation in the shape of British industry competing in international markets gathered pace in the 1970s, leading to the massive shake out of firms in the first four years of the Thatcher government of 1979 and the huge rise in unemployment. In some sectors, ethnic minorities were concentrated among those losing their jobs. In other cases, employment in sectors where Black labour had been on the increase became much less accessible.

Before returning to the distinctive features of the employment situation of Caribbeans and South Asians in Britain to see how far this interpretation of broad economic processes of change can be used to support the picture shown, it is useful to consider briefly four additional points concerning how ethnic minorities might respond to their increasingly marginal economic position: what opportunities have newly created jobs offered, how far can education and training provide entry to jobs in the new economic context, what potential is there in the public sector to provide economic opportunities and how far can an ethnic business sector provide an alternative economic ladder? It is beyond the scope of this chapter to deal with these topics in detail but it is useful to consider their role in constructing a framework to interpret the economic situation of ethnic minorities.

First, while millions of jobs have been lost to the UK economy in recent years, it can be argued that millions of new jobs have likewise been created. However, it is crucial, in assessing their potential for providing new economic opportunities for ethnic minorities, to consider the nature of the employment created. To begin with, many of the new jobs have required advanced knowledge, frequently supported by formal qualifications, which are outside the reach of those made redundant. In many cases, again, even when the level of knowledge or experience required makes them accessible to the casualties of economic contraction in the 1980s, the firms creating employment are located in areas well away from the centres of industrial concentration where ethnic minorities have settled. Of the jobs created in urban-industrial areas, however, many consist of part-time employment unsuited to the needs of ethnic minorities. In practice, the choice for many of those entering the job market or looking for work in mid career in industrial areas without advanced formal qualifications is between unemployment or accepting low wage work in one of the new service industries which are not facing international competition and can make intensive use of cheap labour to deliver their services.

Secondly, there are opportunities for those still at school or entering the labour force to acquire the education, training and qualifications needed to bid for the high quality employment being created. Indeed, the high level of students among those aged 16–24 years of an ethnic minority background suggests that this opportunity is being seized. For example, the proportion of West Indians (18 per cent) in this group classified as students in the Labour Force Survey is almost half as high again as the figure for Whites (13 per cent), while the proportions of Indians (32 per cent) and Pakistanis and Bangladeshis (30 per cent) are three times as high (Department of Employment, 1988). Interestingly, among Whites there is no significant gender difference in the proportion of students, among Asians males are very much more likely to be students and among West Indians females are somewhat more likely to be students. However, there is a far from automatic correlation between student status and eventual employment in a high level position. Among those in post-school training schemes, too, there are many factors which mediate this relationship, not least the concentration of White school leavers in the category of training most likely to be offered good quality work and the tendency noted in studies to associate ethnic minority school leavers with the need for corrective training in attitudes (Cross, 1987). Thus, while ethnic minority school leavers have much to gain from pursuing higher and further education or vocational training, the return to these investments in human capital, whether through features of the education/training or of the subsequent selection process, may fall short of expectation.

Thirdly, given the readiness of public bodies, notably local authorities, to declare themselves equal opportunity employers, it may be argued that there are relatively better opportunities for ethnic minorities in public sector employment. In the USA, for example, Blacks have been over-represented in public sector jobs while remaining under-represented in the private sector (Bailey and Waldinger, 1988). Indeed, there are many examples of local authorities who have taken action to increase the proportion from ethnic minorities among their employees. However, there is little to suggest that this is having a significant impact on their employment prospects. Vacancies only occur when staff are being replaced or new jobs created and, given pressures on the public sector in recent years, there have in all probability been insufficient vacancies, especially in high level positions, to have a noticeable effect, even assuming the availability of qualified ethnic minority candidates and an absence of racial bias in recruitment. In practice, informal processes which serve to maintain the employment of particular ethnic or social groups operate in the public as well as the private sector.

Finally, self-employment has in recent years been enthusiastically supported as an avenue of economic opportunity open to those unable to find paid work. Furthermore, there is a widespread assumption that this is an area where Asians in particular have a natural advantage. However, both these views are highly misleading unless they are put within context. For example, in 1977, fifteen years after the end of unrestricted immigration from the New Commonwealth, the rate of self-employment among household heads from India and Pakistan was no higher than for the general population (National Dwelling and Household Survey, quoted in Ward, 1987b, p. 160). Similarly, in the USA, the business participation rate among Asian Indians has been much lower than that for many European ancestry groups (ibid, p. 163). It was only after the recession of the late 1970s/early 1980s that Asian business achieved any statistical significance in Britain, and much of it has been accurately portrayed by Aldrich and his colleagues (1982, 1984) as a precarious attempt to make a living less rewarding than paid employment. Admittedly, Indians in Britain show a high level of self-employment and a level of unemployment only half as high again as that of Whites. Yet Pakistanis and Bangladeshis have the highest rate of self-employment of all minorities identified in the Labour Force Survey (23 per cent) and also the highest unemployment rate (31 per cent, compared to 10 per cent for Whites) (Department of Employment, 1988, pp. 167,177). While Asian business, therefore, has allowed many to avoid unemployment, there are very many others for whom it has not provided an economic livelihood, either in the form of business ownership or a job in an ethnic firm. Finally, levels of self-employment among Asians in Britain are above average, among West Indians they are below average.

Thus, the lesson to be drawn from the pattern of ethnic business is that, as with small businesses in general, it is only successful in particular contexts which favour its development. The networks of interdependent Asian firms in the clothing trade show some of the success characteristics of their counterparts in industrial districts in Italy (Werbner, 1984; Bamford, 1987; Ward, 1987a). But much Asian business disguises the continuing reality of economic disadvantage.

APPLICATION

The interpretation of economic change and its impact on ethnic minority communities fits well with the pattern of ethnic differentiation described above.

First, the continuing concentration of ethnic minorities in the industrial regions and areas of original settlement where they have borne the brunt of economic retrenchment can be interpreted in terms of a lack of qualification for many of the jobs being created elsewhere, restricted access to such jobs where they were competing with local Whites, difficulties in moving house to new areas and a preference for seeking whatever economic livelihood could be obtained from a base within the ethnic community.

Secondly, the substantially higher unemployment experienced by all ethnic minorities in all regions and areas shows the universality of racial disadvantage at work in the general response to the restructuring of employment. While there are highly significant inter-ethnic differentials in the level of unemployment which suggest that particular communities have adopted distinctive methods of coping with economic crisis, the single clearest differentiating factor in the economic position of West Indians and Asians compared to Whites is the higher level of unemployment among a population of migrants (with their children) who came to Britain to find work. It is hard to avoid seeing, in this pattern, the systematic racial bias shown in detailed studies of racial discrimination in employment (Smith, 1977; Brown, 1984; Brown and Gay, 1985). However, the distinctive position of all ethnic minorities identified shows that racial disadvantage is very unevenly experienced and is highly contingent on factors specific to particular groups and locations. In particular, the gulf between unemployment levels among Indians and Pakistanis/Bangladeshis shows the dangers of defining a generalized 'Asian' orientation to ways of making a living and shows the continuing significance of class and class-related differences in coming to terms with the realities of economic processes in Britain (Nowikowski, 1984).

Thirdly, in contrast to the overall differences in unemployment rates,

ethnic differences in level of employment are much less clear-cut. This, together with the pattern of inter-ethnic differences, suggests that within the
place of employment, opportunities depend far more on socio-economic and
other distinctions than the quest for a job.

Finally, the greatest complexity is found when gender is brought into the
analysis, giving further support to the view that the experience of racial disadvantage is heavily conditioned by factors internal to particular ethnic
minorities. The lesser impact of unemployment on men among Asians may
reflect the gender-specific path of ethnic business development. Among those
from the Caribbean, the fact that women suffer less from unemployment may
be related to their greater involvement in education, but both may reflect
more basic features of economic opportunity structures. Further interesting
inter-ethnic differences are found when gender is combined with area of residence. The higher level of unemployment among Indian women in dispersed
locations suggests that a considerable proportion of their jobs are generated
within Indian communities and related business networks. The fact that
Afro-Caribbeans are much less affected by unemployment away from established centres of the ethnic community points to a much more individualistic
method of obtaining employment which is more successful in low concentration areas, in part no doubt a function of differences in qualifications.

Again, the closer match between the levels of employment among women
in different ethnic groups raises interesting questions about gender-specific
dimensions of the impact of racial disadvantage. Gender based differences
between ethnic groups also call for explanation. The above average level of
employment among Pakistani/Bangladeshi women presumably reflects the
tendency for women of lower social status not to be economically active. But
the same phenomenon among Afro-Caribbeans occurs despite a high level of
labour force participation among women.

CONCLUSION

This chapter has sought to describe and interpret the reality of paid work
among the ethnic minority population in Britain in terms of a broad overview
of economic processes over recent decades. It has been outside the scope of
the chapter to review the large body of detailed analysis concerning ethnic
differentiation in particular types of employment. Our concern has been
much more to demonstrate the essential inter-relatedness of different contributing factors. The statistical pattern of racial disadvantage in employment
is strongly suggestive of the continuing existence of racial discrimination as
confirmed elsewhere. Its impact, however, depends upon a number of con-
textual factors. Among these, the types (and quantities) of jobs created compared to those lost are clearly of great importance. This gives rise to *socio-
economic* explanations which emphasize the polarization of employment
into high-level knowledge based jobs beyond the reach of many of those from

ethnic minorities in the labour market and low pay, low skill jobs in the service economy. The implications of this approach are, as Cross (1989) has observed, to concentrate on better education and training and more effective welfare support as ways of reducing the impact of racial disadvantage in employment.

There is a separate approach, however, which focuses on the *spatial effects* of economic change and the locational distribution of employment. This emphasis, too, is given support by the statistical pattern set out above. The implications of this line of analysis are quite different, away from welfare support which ties the poor into areas where their prospects are worst towards the encouragement of geographical mobility to areas of employment growth. This is not a blandishment to ethnic minorities to get on their bikes; rather it is a recognition that state sponsored support, such as employment training, might be more closely tied to real job prospects.

Both these approaches need to be complemented by a recognition of the dynamics of *ethnic differentiation*. All ethnic minorities were not in the same employment position from the outset, and the process of economic restructuring has tended to make their paths diverge still more. It is too early to say whether the division within the 'Asian' communities between Indians and Pakistani/Bangladeshis is one which will narrow in time, as educational performance data suggest, or whether Afro-Caribbeans and some poor Asians share the same economic fate. Some have argued for the former view, which generates the prospect that the employment future for those of Caribbean origin in the UK is of critical importance (Cross and Johnson 1988). It is not inconceivable that we may be witnessing the development of an urban 'underclass' at precisely the same time that economic fortunes overall are improving (Wilson, 1987).

What is undoubtedly true is that attempts to devise policies which are effective in reducing racial disadvantage in employment need to pay close attention to the internal dynamics within particular ethnic communities (and sub-communities), and to gaining an understanding of the socio-economic and spatial effects of economic change, as well as to more direct policies of combating racial discrimination.

9
Disability and participation in the labour market

MIKE OLIVER

INTRODUCTION

There is no doubt that since the end of the Second World War, the proportion of disabled people who have been unemployed has been consistently higher than it has been for the rest of the population (Buckle, 1971; Townsend, 1979; Lonsdale and Walker 1980). In terms of labour market participation there are four areas where it is generally agreed that disabled people fare worse than everyone else (Townsend 1981, p. 58):

1 Fewer are employed
2 Fewer have high earnings and more have low earnings
3 More hours tend to be worked to secure the same earnings
4 Slightly fewer have good conditions of work.

The evidence to support these assertions will not be discussed in any detail in this Chapter precisely because there is broad agreement on the general thrust of these points. The only specific issues that are at stake are the problems of dealing with unreliable statistical data and precisely what percentage of disabled people are actually unemployed or under-employed.

There are some generalizations that can be made, however, to demonstrate the extent of discrimination against disabled people in the labour market. A recent Government survey (Martin, White and Meltzer, 1989) showed that, of the 2 million disabled people of working age in the country, only 31 per cent are in paid employment. While not all of the rest are actively seeking work, Lonsdale (1986) estimated that when the unemployment rate amongst the general population was 19.2 per cent, it was 50.1 per cent of the disabled population. In a recent debate in the House of Commons (Hansard, 6 June 1989), the situation was summarized thus:

When we look at the question of unemployment amongst disabled people we find that not only are they discriminated against, not only are they the people who are most likely to be without a job, but they are also the ones who are most likely to be without a job for the longest time. Whereas only 8 per cent of non-disabled people have been jobless for more than two years, no less than 26 per cent of disabled job seekers have been jobless for more than two years. (col. 69)

In the same debate it was pointed out that the average weekly earnings of male full-time workers was £192.40, the average for disabled male full-time workers was £156.70; that is, only 81 per cent of average earnings.

As a consequence of this, disabled people are trapped in a situation of unemployment, underemployment and poverty (Townsend, 1979; Martin, White and Meltzer 1989). Whether this means that disabled people constitute an underclass in society is a difficult question to answer, particularly as the value of the concept of an underclass is still being debated within sociology. Here it will be argued that disabled people do constitute an underclass for two reasons. First, it can be shown that disabled people are in an inferior position to other social groups, including the working class, in terms of housing (Borsay, 1986), employment (Lonsdale, 1986), finance (Martin and White, 1989), transport (Hoad, 1986) and education (Anderson, 1979). Secondly, disabled people have been denied access to key political, educational and cultural institutions which could enable them to participate fully in society (Oliver, 1990). Hence, it can be stated that they constitute an underclass rather than a sub-strata of the working class. This issue will be returned to later but in the meantime, it is necessary to point out that disabled people have become an underclass, not because of their perceived or real physical limitations, but because changes in the work system have excluded them from the work process. This exclusion has had profound effects on social relations as well, resulting not just in the marginalization of the disabled within labour markets, but from society as a whole. To put the matter simply, an underclass has been created by society rather than produced by the characteristics of this particular group.

The crucial issue to be discussed here is why this should be so, and it will be argued that it is the changing needs of the labour market rather than the limitations (perceived or real) of disabled workers which has produced this situation. In order to understand how this has happened, it will be necessary to examine historical changes in the work process that came about with the rise of capitalism, and which resulted not simply in the marginalization of disabled people within labour markets but from society as a whole. This marginalization has made the disabled part of an underclass and the implications of this will be considered in the light of the new possibilities opened up by the rise of new technologies. Finally, the issue of social change through the emergence of a new politics of disability will be discussed.

CONCEPTUAL FRAMEWORK

Before proceeding to discuss these issues in detail, it is necessary to consider the changes that definitions of disability have undergone in recent times. Traditionally, because of the dominant position of the medical profession, disability has been defined in terms of clinical conditions such as arthritis, multiple sclerosis, stroke, epilepsy, spinal injury and so on. However, the limitations of such definitions have been recognized in that they do not take account of the social dimensions of disability which can be crucial when providing services rather than just medical treatments. Thus, for example, the Disabled Persons (Employment) Act 1944 set out to provide services for disabled adults who were 'substantially handicapped by mental or physical disability in finding and keeping employment'. When, in the 1960s, the Government was considering policy initiatives in respect of disability, it commissioned the Office of Population Censuses and Surveys (OPCS) to undertake a national survey to ascertain the numbers of disabled in the country. OPCS, in carrying out this task, attempted to operationalize the social dimension of disability by proposing a threefold distinction upon the following lines:

- *Impairment* – Any loss or abnormality of psychological, physiological or anatomical structure or function.
- *Disability* – any restriction or lack of ability (resulting from an impairment) to perform an activity in the manner or within the range considered normal for a human being.
- *Handicap* – a disadvantage for a given individual, resulting from an impairment or disability, that limits or prevents the fulfilment of a role that is normal, depending upon age, sex, social and cultural factors, for that individual.

This schema, with slight modifications, has formed the basis for the International Classification of Impairments, Disabilities and Handicaps published by the World Health Organization in 1981 and the subsequent second national survey of disabled adults in Britain (Martin and White, 1989). These definitions have not been without their critics, notably disabled people, who have argued that they are ultimately 'victim blaming' in that the causes of disability are reduced to the impairment of individuals. In addition, these definitions reify the notions of physical normality and normal social roles. (For fuller discussion of these issues see Oliver, 1990).

As a consequence of this the Union of the Physically Impaired Against Segregation suggested its own definition of disability as 'the disadvantage or restriction of activity caused by a contemporary social organization which takes no or little account of people who have physical impairments and thus excludes them from the mainstream of social activities'. Subsequently, Disabled People's International challenged the World Health Organization with its own re-definition as 'the loss or limitation of opportunities to take part in the life of the community on an equal level with others due to physical and social barriers'.

These definitions see disability as a social restriction rather than individual limitation, and it is this framework which will be adopted in this Chapter. Thus no attempt will be made to categorize disabled people by clinical conditions or functional limitations on the grounds that all disabled people experience disability as social restriction. That is not to deny that the degree of social restriction may differ depending upon clinical condition or functional limitation, but to assert that these differences are less important than the commonalities imposed on the experience of disability by social restriction.

THE MODE OF PRODUCTION AND HISTORICAL CHANGE

Work is central to all societies not simply because it produces the goods to sustain life but also because it creates particular forms of social relations. Thus anyone unable to work, for whatever reason, is likely to experience difficulties both in acquiring the necessities to sustain life physically, and also in establishing a set of satisfactory social relationships. To put the matter simply in respect of disability, restricted mobility is likely to create greater difficulties in nomadic societies than in agricultural ones. Blind people are far more likely to face exclusion from work processes based upon complex hand–eye co-ordination than in those based upon craft skills. And in terms of social relations, disabled people are less likely to face social exclusion in societies where roles such as 'beggar' or 'village idiot' are acceptable, than in those where they are not.

Clearly the most significant change that has occurred with regard to the work process and the effect that this had on disabled people was the coming of industrial society, or to put it slightly differently, the transition from feudalism to capitalism. It was Marx and his theory of historical materialism who has contributed most to our understanding of the general implications of these changes. His view has been summarized by Forder *et al.* (1984) as:

> the relationship between people, their work and their environment is to be related to the socio-economic structure of society. So an understand-ing of historical process makes possible an understanding of human nature and the social relationships which exist at any particular point in time. (p. 89)

Thus, in understanding the social relations that constitute disability as social restriction, the changes that occurred in the work process with the coming of industrial society, are clearly crucial.

But historical materialism is not just about placing social relationships within a historical setting. It also attempts to provide an evolutionary perspective on human history, of particular relevance here are the transitions from feudal through capitalist to socialist society. No attempt has been made to apply this (or indeed any other social theory) to the history of disability. However, Finkelstein (1980, 1981) has located such an account within a materialist framework and developed an evolutionary model – broadly along the lines of the three stages of the historical materialist model mentioned above – although without using the same terminology.

His model is couched in terms of three phases of historical development. Phase 1 corresponds to Britain before the industrial revolution; that is feudal society. Phase 2 corresponds to the process of industrialization when the focus of work shifted from the home to the factory; that is capitalist society. This takes us up to the present day, and Phase 3 refers to the kind of society to which we are currently moving, though Finkelstein does not spell out the differences between Phases 2 and 3, nor does he comment on whether Phase 3 marks the beginning of the transition to socialism as predicted by historical materialism.

The economic base in Phase 1, agriculture or small-scale industry, did not preclude the great majority of disabled people from participating in the production process and even where they could not participate fully they were still able to make a contribution. In this era disabled people were regarded as individually unfortunate and not segregated from the rest of society. With the rise of the factory in Phase 2, many more disabled people were excluded from the production process (Ryan and Thomas, 1980) for:

> The speed of factory work, the enforced discipline, the time-keeping and production norms – all these were a highly unfavourable change from the slower, more self-determined and flexible methods of work into which many handicapped people had been integrated. (p. 101)

As capitalism developed, this process of exclusion from the work-force continued for all kinds of disabled people (Topliss, 1979):

> By the 1890's, the population of Britain was increasingly urban and the employment of the majority was industrial, rather than rural. The blind and the deaf growing up in slowly changing scattered rural communities had more easily been absorbed into the work and life of those societies without the need for special provision. Deafness, while working alone at agricultural tasks that all children learned by observation with little formal schooling, did not limit the capacity for employment too severely. Blindness was less of a hazard in uncongested familiar rural surroundings, and routine tasks involving repetitive tactile skills could be learned and practiced by many of the blind without special training. The environment of an industrial society was however different. (p. 11)

Changes in the organization of work from a rural based, co-operative system where individuals contributed what they could to the production process, to an urban, factory based one organized around the individual waged labourer, had profound consequences (Morris, 1969):

> The operation of the labour market in the nineteenth century effectively depressed handicapped people of all kinds to the bottom of the market. (p. 9)

As a result of this, disabled people came to be regarded as a social and educational problem and more and more were segregated in institutions of all kinds including workhouses, asylums, colonies and special schools, and out of the mainstream of social life. The emergence of Phase 3, according to Finkelstein, will see the liberation of disabled people from the segregative practices of society largely as a consequence of the utilization of new technologies and the working together of professionals and disabled people towards common goals. Whether this is likely to be so, is an issue which will be returned to later in this chapter.

For Finkelstein, disability is a paradox involving the state of the individual (his or her impairment) and the state of society (the social restrictions imposed on an individual). By adopting a three-stage evolutionary perspective, he sees the paradox emerging in Phase 2. In Phase 1 disabled individuals formed part of a larger underclass but in Phase 2 they were separated from their class origins and became a special, segregated group, whereby the paradox emerged and disability came to be regarded both as individual impairment and social restriction. Phase 3, which is just beginning, sees the end of the paradox where disability comes to be perceived solely as social restriction.

Like historical materialism this model has explanatory power particularly in helping us to understand what happened in Phase 2 or with the emergence of capitalist society. However, it does tend to over-simplify what was happening prior to this capitalist emergence. It implies that in Phase 1, some kind of idealized community existed and that disabled people, amongst other minority groups, were treated more benignly. It is certainly true that the emergence of capitalism had profound effects on social relations generally and that many acceptable social roles and positions disappeared, and this directly affected disabled people in many instances. It is difficult, however, to assess whether these changes affected the quality of the experience of disability negatively or positively, largely because history is relatively silent on the experience of disability.

A similar model has been advanced to explain variations in social responses to and personal experiences of disability in the modern world (Sokolowska, Ostrowska and Titkow 1981). They suggest that there are three kinds of society in the modern world; what they call developing, intermediary developed and highly developed or types I, II and III. Type I societies are characterized by an underdeveloped economy with few job opportunities for unskilled disabled workers though their spontaneous participation is ensured through the acceptable social roles of 'beggar' and 'pauper'. Type II societies have a developed economy based upon manufacturing and are characterized by the separation of disabled people from the rest of society through a series of specific social policies and because of various architectural and transportation barriers. Type III societies have highly developed economies based upon consumption and are, or should be, characterized by the integration of disabled people, made possible by the supply of 'necessary appliances'.

This contemporary model, like Finkelstein's historical one, is of considerable value in highlighting the importance of the mode of production in significantly influencing perceptions and experiences of disability. However both models are over-simplistic and over-optimistic. They are over-simplistic in that they assume a simple relationship between the mode of production and perceptions and experiences of disability, without considering a range of other influential factors such as the development of welfare provision, the role of ideology and politics and the effects of professional attitudes. They are also too optimistic in that both assume that technological developments will liberate disabled people and integrate them back into society.

In order to better understand this over-simplification and false optimism, it is necessary to bring the debate up to date and consider the effects of the present day work system on social relations as they affect disabled people.

AN ECONOMIC BASIS FOR THE CREATION OF DEPENDENCY

Work is still central to modern industrial societies despite claims that we are moving to post-industrial, post-capitalist or the leisure society, not simply because it produces the goods to sustain life but also because it creates particular forms of social relations. Modern governments however, attempt to intervene in these social relations through various welfare programmes and provisions (for example, National Assistance Act 1948, Chronically Sick and Disabled Persons Act 1970) as well as in the work process itself (Disabled Persons [Employment] Act 1944). There is ample evidence to show that these interventions neither work in terms of influencing social relations (Shearer, 1983) nor in opening up the work system for particular groups (Grover and Gladstone, 1981; Lonsdale and Walker, 1984). Thus, despite such interventions, anyone unable to work, for whatever reason, is likely to experience difficulties both in acquiring the necessities to sustain life physically, and also in establishing a set of satisfactory social relationships.

These interventions have not worked for a variety of reasons and we need to consider some of them here in order to understand why political commitment and social provision has not changed the status of disabled people as an underclass. To begin with, even where attempts are made to influence the work system, they do not have the desired effect because, on the whole, these programmes tend to focus on labour supply. Their aim is to make individual disabled people suitable for work but, while they may succeed in individual cases, such programmes may also have the opposite effect. By packaging and selling them as a special case, the idea that there is something different about disabled workers is reinforced and may be exclusionary rather than inclusionary. But it doesn't have to be this way (Erlanger and Roth, 1985) for:

> The alternative, or more properly the supplement, to these programs is a focus on the demand side of the market, making people more employable and more a part of general social life by changing the social organization of work and of other aspects of everyday life, through removal of architectural barriers, nondiscrimination and affirmative action programs, mainstreaming in the schools, and so on. Until recently, there has been almost no concern with these possibilities. (p. 339)

It could, of course, be argued that government policy aimed at providing aids to employment and the adaptation of workplaces is precisely this approach but it is nothing of the kind. These initiatives are all geared towards the supply side of labour, at making individual disabled people more economically productive and hence more acceptable to employers. There are no government incentives to create barrier-free work environments nor can Ford claim a grant if it wants to make its assembly line usable by all the potential work-force. Neither can other manufacturers wishing to design machinery or tools that are usable by everyone, regardless of their functional abilities, seek government assistance. There are virtually no attempts in modern capitalist societies that are targeted at the social organization of work, that is, at the demand side of labour. And given the size of the reserve pool of labour that currently exists in most capitalist societies, it is unlikely that such targeting will occur in the foreseeable future.

In order to understand why government interventions in the area of social relations have not worked either, it is necessary to return to the onset of industrial society. The new mechanism for controlling economically unproductive people was the workhouse or the asylum, and over the years a whole range of specialized institutions grew up to contain this group. These establishments were undoubtedly successful in controlling individuals who would not or could not work. They also performed a particular ideological function, standing as visible monuments to the fate of others who might no longer choose to subjugate themselves to the disciplinary requirements of the new work system. There were problems too in that it was soon recognized that these institutions not only created dependency in individuals but also created dependent groups. This led to fears about the 'burdens of pauperism' in the early twentieth century and the establishment of the Poor Law Commission. Similar concerns are around today, although the language is different and current moves towards community care have strong economic motives underpinning them.

Part of this economic motivation centres on a desire to reduce public expenditure on groups of people perceived to be dependent; the restructuring of welfare provision in the 1980s has been facilitated by an ideology which suggests we have created a 'dependency culture'. It is argued that dependency has been created by the very policies that were designed to alleviate it and recent policy changes have attempted to withdraw support from these dependent groups by a range of measures such as privatization, contracting out and targeting.

The problem with this argument is that it is reductionist; it treats the concept of dependency as a non-problematic one seeking to divide the population into two groups, the dependent and the independent, and in so doing, it fails to acknowledge that everyone in modern, industrial societies lives in a state of 'mutual dependency' (Oliver, 1990). It is also reductionist in that it focuses on the common characteristics of different groups (for example, old people, disabled people, people with mental illnesses and so on), of which enforced dependency is a major feature, and applies the blanket label 'dependent' to them all without any consideration of how this dependency is created or any significant differences between the labelled groups.

Given the historical and current situation it is hardly surprising that such uncritical sociological reductionism can characterize disabled people and other groups as follows (Illsley, 1981):

> Their condition or situation makes them economically unproductive and hence economically and socially dependent. (p. 328)

This is only partly true, however, for despite the high rates of unemployment in the industrialized world, many disabled people of working age do have a job, and hence are economically productive. In addition, day centres, adult training centres and sheltered workshops make a considerable economic contribution by carrying out jobs that cannot easily be mechanized at wage rates that make third world workers look expensive.

But more importantly, this takes a narrow view of the economy and fails to recognize the importance of consumption. At present the benefits paid to disabled people amount to almost seven billion pounds a year (Disability Alliance, 1987) most of which 'will almost invariable be spent to the full' (George and Wilding, 1984). The numbers of firms now producing aids and equipment for disabled people and the seriousness with which motor manufacturers now take disabled motorists are testament to the important and 'productive' role that disabled people play in the economy of late capitalism; that is, an economy driven by consumption.

Following Illsley's narrow definition, the British Royal Family can be characterized as economically unproductive and economically and socially dependent. However, it is recognized that the institution of the Monarchy performs an important economic role and they are not labelled 'dependants', except by their fiercest critics. That disabled people can be so labelled therefore, is due to a variety of other factors and is not solely a function of inaccurate assumptions about their role in the economy. A major factor in this labelling of disabled people as unproductive is that of power; disabled people as an underclass lack the political power to challenge such labels through the traditional political system of party or interest group politics (Oliver and Zarb, 1989). Also, as an underclass, they lack the social status which prevents such labelling from happening, which is clearly different in the case of the Royal Family.

These policies are also doomed to failure precisely because they attempt to adjust these social relations in isolation, rather than attempt to deal with the way the work system actually creates dependency within these very social relations (Oliver, 1990). At a policy level, this can be characterized as follows (Walker, 1984):

> Social policy has been assigned. . . . to the role of intervening in a natural order of economic relationships to modify their outcome in the interests of 'social' goals. In both capitalist and state socialist societies, social policy has operated as a 'handmaiden' to the economy. (p. 33)

The analysis so far suggests that disabled people as an underclass are unlikely to have their social position improved by current government interventions, both because policies in the economic sphere are aimed at the supply rather than demand side of the labour market, and that policies in the social sphere ignore the economic basis of dependency creation. But what of the future? Will the onset of post-capitalist society with all the economic and social changes that it will bring, see improvements in the status of disabled people to the point where they can no longer be called an underclass?

POST-CAPITALISM AND THE DISAPPEARANCE OF THE DISABLED UNDERCLASS?

A major factor to be considered in the development of post-capitalist society is the influence of new technological developments on the economic, social and material needs of disabled people. Finkelstein (1980), while not specifically calling Phase 3 of his model post-capitalism, is clear where both the problem and the solution, lies:

> Disabled people, also, no less than able-bodied people, need to express their essential human nature by moulding the social and material environment and so influence the course of history. What stands in the way, (at a time when the material and technological basis for solving the human and material needs of disabled people have mostly been solved), is the dominance of phase 2 attitudes and relationships. Such attitudes take society and, indeed, the dependency relationship as given. (p. 39)

But not all commentators see the issue as one of out-dated attitudes moulding technology in particular directions, but point to the fact that technology itself will not necessarily produce or equally distribute its benefits (Habermas, 1971; Illich, 1973). These technological developments have not been universally welcomed in terms of health care in general (Reiser, 1978; Taylor, 1979) nor disability in particular (Oliver, 1978). Zola (1982), writing from his own experience has suggested that:

> Technology can do too much for those of us with disabilities. The machines that technology creates may achieve such completeness that they rob us of our integrity by making us feel useless. (p. 395)

And he applies this analysis not just to the development of machines, gadgets and prostheses, but also to what he calls 'the over-technicalization of care'.

> To be handled by a machine or animal, where once I was handled by a person, can only be invalidating of me as a person. (p. 396)

Further, in terms of its effects on the work system and the material and social environments, it may be oppressive rather than liberating. In a review of changes in the work system in what he calls 'post-industrial society', Cornes (1988) discusses both the optimistic and pessimistic views of the effects of new technology on the work opportunities of disabled people. He suggests that such developments can be viewed optimistically:

> New jobs and new opportunities to organise and locate work on an entirely different basis using new technologies are increasingly being perceived as offering even more grounds for optimism. This is because such new jobs, in which physical requirements are replaced by electronic skill, strength and precision are particularly suitable for people with disabilities, and because new developments in communications have increased opportunities for home-based employment. (p. 15)

But he then sounds a cautionary note, suggesting that many disabled people may not have the educational opportunities or training potential to take advantage of such opportunities. Furthermore, the new skills that will be required to master new technology may require a degree of confidence and independent thinking that many disabled people currently lack. Finally, he suggests that many disabled people are already falling behind in the mastery of these skills 'because of problems of access, mobility, finance and discriminatory attitudes'.

He agrees with Finkelstein's (1980) analysis, that the problem is that while we are in phase 3 in terms of economic and technological developments, we none the less, remain locked into phase 2 attitudes, or in his terms, that 'existing policies, programmes, attitudes and expectations may be too dependent on the institutional arrangements, values and ideals of an industrial society' (Cornes 1988). And he goes on to locate the solution as being in the hands of the disability movement itself:

> Their successful participation in all spheres of life within post-industrial society – economic, cultural and political – will depend greatly on the extent to which they themselves and their supporters can lay claim to and exercise the right not only during the transition from school to work but throughout their lifetimes. (p. 17)

There is nothing in this analysis to suggest that the rise of new technologies within post-capitalism will bring about fundamental changes in the work system and hence automatically create opportunities for disabled people to participate fully. Indeed, the implication is that such opportunities will only materialize if disabled people themselves can act to ensure their full participation in both the work system and contingent social relations.

A NEW POLITICS OF DISABILITY

Given that traditional political activity takes place within the party system or through pressure group activity, and that disabled people are denied full participation in both (Borsay, 1986; Fry, 1987; Oliver and Zarb, 1989), then new kinds of political activity need to be developed. As has already been argued, disabled people are an underclass in that they are marginalized within the work-force, suffer exclusion in social relations, and lack political power and social status. A major reason for this is that disabled people are not a single, unitary group (Oliver, 1984):

> To begin with there is a great deal of variety within the disabled population as a whole – differences in social class, age, sex, family circumstances and clinical conditions – as well as the fact that disability may have developed after political commitments had been established. In addition, many disabled people do not necessarily regard themselves as disabled, or even if they do, would not contemplate joining an organisation for disabled people. Finally, as a consequence of disability, some people may disengage from political activity, either because their physical impairment poses limitations of a physical or psychological kind, or because they are aware that in many contexts they lack any basis for exercising power, e.g. through the withdrawal of their labour. (p. 23)

Extending this analysis, it has also been suggested that the medical approach to disability has fostered artificial divisions within the disabled population (Borsay, 1986). But these divisions do not arise simply from the medical approach, for the State also provides services in such a way as to foster divisions within the disabled population. Hence, it gives tax allowances to blind people but not to other categories of disability, mobility allowances to those who cannot walk but not for those who can, and higher pensions and benefits for those injured at work or in the services than for those with congenital disabilities or those who have had accidents. This is not an unintentional consequence of State provision but a deliberate tactic which the State has developed in its dealings with other groups and can be summed up as 'divide and rule'.

This idea of disabled people as a group divided amongst itself has obvious implications for any notions of class based political activity (Funk, 1987):

> The myriad of disability-specific programs and policies, the segregation of disabled people, the inability to gain access to organised society, to experience an integrated and adequate education, to obtain meaningful employment, and to socially interact and participate has resulted in a politically powerless and diffuse class of people who are unable to coalesce with other groups of disabled people on common issues, to vote, to be seen or heard. This class has accepted the stigma and caste of second-hand citizenship and the incorrect judgement of social inferiority. (p. 24)

This judgement is somewhat harsh and outdated, for the 1980s have seen the rise of an increasingly strong and vibrant disability movement at local, national and international levels (Oliver, 1984; Ryan, 1988) which is beginning to have an impact on policy formulation, welfare provision and professional practice. In addition it is engaged with society in ideological confrontations about the nature and meaning of disability (Finkelstein, 1980) as well as the technological rationality underpinning post-capitalism. For example, there is a recognition that the mentality which allows technology to be used for evil purposes is the very same mentality which facilitates the oppression (and indeed, even the creation) of disabled people (Davis, 1986):

> Relentlessly, the connection between disability and the bomb becomes clear. The mentality that made Cheshire a compliant participant in the mass creation of disability at Hiroshima is the same mentality which made him the instigator of the mass incarceration of disabled people in a chain of segregated institutions. In the first case he went over the tops of the heads of disabled people in a B29 bomber, in the second he went over our heads in the name of charity. Increasingly, over the years, both actions have come to attract our abhorrence . . . we have to find the strength to *INSIST* that our representative organisations are fully involved in decisions about the dismantling of disabled apartheid. And we have to add our INSTANT voice to the clamour for WORLD DISARMAMENT – with the aim of removing for all time, this particular and horrifying cause of unnecessary disability. (p. 3)

But, in order to challenge what might be called attitudes (Finkelstein, 1980, 1981; Cornes, 1988), mentality (Davis, 1986) or more properly, in the context of this analysis, ideology, then clearly the disability movement must work out an appropriate political strategy. One of the features of post-capitalist society has been the emergence of many new social movements comprising of neighbourhood groups, environmentalists, welfare recipients, the unemployed, minority groups and the 'generally disenfranchised' (Castells, 1978; Touraine, 1981; Boggs, 1986). These movements have been seen as constituting the social basis for new forms of transformative political action or change and they are new in the sense that they are not grounded in traditional forms of political participation. In short, we have seen the rise of a new politics of the underclasses and the disability movement is clearly one strand in this new politics.

There is not the time or space to consider in detail the significance of new social movements in general (Laclau and Mouffe, 1985) or the disability movement in particular (Oliver and Zarb, 1989; Oliver, 1990). However, the relationship of the disability movement to organized labour does need to be briefly considered within the context of

> The complex relationship between labour and social movements, class and politics – not to mention the recomposition of the work force itself – invalidates any scheme that assigns to labour a hegemonic or privileged role in social transformation. (Boggs, 1986, p. 233)

Thus it is clear that the disability movement cannot look to organized labour as the main vehicle for opening up the work system and enabling them to participate fully. Up to now, while organized labour has been broadly supportive in wishing to retain the Quota, established by the Disabled Persons (Employment) Act 1944, it has been notably resistant to changing work practices to facilitate the employment of disabled people and to re-writing job specifications to enable disabled people to get the kind of personal support they need to lead better lives both in the community and in residential care.

Finally, in considering these new social movements it has to be admitted that nowhere in the world have they been successful in bringing about fundamental changes. Their significance has been in placing new issues onto the political agenda, in presenting old issues in new forms and indeed, in opening up new areas of political discourse. It is, perhaps, their counter-hegemonic potential, not their actual achievements, that are significant in post-capitalist society (Boggs, 1986):

> To say that the new movements have counter-hegemonic potential is also to suggest that they have emerged in opposition (at least partially) to those ideologies that legitimate the power structure; technological rationality, nationalism, competitive individualism, and, of course, racism and sexism. (p. 243)

Thus, the ideology of disablism must also be challenged for only then can we conceive of the possibility of disabled people no longer confined to the role of an underclass within post-capitalist society.

In conclusion, this chapter has suggested that disabled people are, by and large, excluded from labour market participation not because of their own, perceived or real, physical incapacities, but because of changes in the work process which occurred with the coming of industrial capitalist society. This has resulted in the marginalization of disabled people from all aspects of society and placed them in the position of an underclass. It has further been argued that there are limited grounds for optimism in the rise of new technologies which are being developed within present day, post-capitalist society and that this optimism is dependent upon the extent to which disabled people themselves can advance their own claims for full participation in society, including the work process. Finally, the advancement of such claims is dependent upon the extent to which new social movements in general, and the disability movement in particular, can influence changes in economic and social policies, which may, in turn, result in the full participation of disabled people in all aspects of life, including labour markets, and hence, successfully challenge their current status as an underclass.

References

ACAS (1988). *Labour Flexibility in Britain: The 1987 ACAS Survey*, Occasional Paper 41, ACAS.

Albrecht, G. (ed.) (1981). *Cross National Rehabilitation Policies: A Sociological Perspective*. London: Sage.

Aldrich, H., Cater, J., Jones, T. and McEvoy, D. (1982). 'From periphery to peripheral: the South Asian petite bourgeoisie in England', in Simpson, I. H. and Simpson, R. (eds), *Research in the Sociology of Work*, vol. 2. Greenwich, Ct.: JAI Press.

Aldrich, H., Jones, T. and McEvoy, D. (1984). 'Ethnic advantage and minority business development', in Ward, R. and Jenkins, R. (eds), *Ethnic Communities in Business*. Cambridge: Cambridge University Press.

Allatt, P. and Yeadle, S. (1986). 'It's not fair is it?: youth unemployment, family relations and the social contract', in Allen, S., Watson, A., Purcell, K. and Wood, S. (eds), *The Experience of Unemployment*. London: Macmillan.

Allen, J. and Massey, D. (eds) (1988). *The Economy in Question*. London: Sage.

Allen, S. and Wolkowitz, C. (1987). *Homeworking: Myths and Realities*. London: Macmillan.

Anderson, E. (1979). *The Disabled Schoolchild*. London: Methuen.

Ascher, K. (1987). *The Politics of Privatisation: Contracting Out of the Public Services*. London: Macmillan.

Ashton, D. N. (1986). *Unemployment Under Capitalism*. Brighton: Wheatsheaf.

Ashton, D. and Maguire, M. (1986). *Young Adults in the Labour Market*, Research Paper No. 55. London: Department of Employment.

Ashton, D., Maguire, M. and Spilsbury, M. (1990). *Restructuring the Labour Market: the Implications for Youth*. London, Basingstoke: Macmillan.

Atkinson, J. (1984a). 'Manpower strategies for flexible organisations', *Personnel Management*, August.

Atkinson, J. (1984b). *Flexibility, Uncertainty and Manpower Management*, IMS Report No. 89. Brighton: Institute of Manpower Studies.

Atkinson, J. (1985). *Early Retirement*. IMS Report No. 94. University of Sussex, Institute of Manpower Studies.

Atkinson, J. S. (1987). 'Flexibility or fragmentation? The United Kingdom labour market in the eighties', *Labour and Society*, vol. **12**, no.1.

Auletta, K. (1982) *The Underclass*. New York: Random House.

Bailey, T. and Waldinger, R. (1988). 'Economic change and the ethnic division of labor in New York City', Paper presented for the SSRC Committee on New York City, Dual City Project.

Bamford, J. (1987). 'The development of small firms: the traditional family and agrarian patterns in Italy', in Goffee, R. and Scase, R. (eds), *Entrepreneurship in Europe*. London: Croom Helm.

Banks, M. H. and Ullah, P. (1988). *Youth Unemployment in the 1980s: ICS Psychological Effects*. London: Croom Helm.

Barnett, C. (1986). *The Audit of War: the Illusion and Reality of Britain as a Great Nation*. London, Basingstoke: Macmillan.

Barron, R. D. and Norris, G. M. (1976). 'Sexual divisions and the dual labour market', in D. L. Barker and S. Allen (eds) *Dependence and Exploitation in Work and Marriage*, 47–69. London: Longman.

Batstone, E. and Gourlay, S. (1986). *Unions, Unemployment and Innovation*. Oxford: Basil Blackwell.

Becker, G. (1981). *A Treatise on the Family*. Cambridge: Harvard University Press.

Beechey, V. (1987). *Unequal Work*. London: Verso.

Beechey, V. and Perkins, T. (1987). *A Matter of Hours*. Oxford: Polity.

Ben-David, J. (1966). 'The growth of the professions in the class system', in Bendix, R. and Lipset, S. (eds), *Class, Status and Power*. New York: Free Press.

Beynon, H. (1973). *Working for Ford*. Harmondsworth: Penguin.

Blood, R. O. and Wolfe, D. M. (1960). *Husbands and Wives*. Glencoe: Free Press.

Boggs, C. (1986). *Social Movements and Political Power*. Philadelphia: Temple University Press.

Booth, C. (1984). *The Aged Poor in England and Wales*. London, Basingstoke: Macmillan.

Booth, C. (1887). The inhabitants of the Tower Hamlets (School Board Division), their condition and occupations', *Journal of the Royal Statistical Society*, vol. **L**.

Booth, C. (1902). *Life and Labour of the People of London* (17 volumes). London: Macmillan.

Borsay, A. (1986). *Disabled People in the Community*. London: Bedford Square Press.

Bowers, J., Deaton, D. and Turk, J. (1982). *Labour Hoarding in British Industry*. Oxford: Basil Blackwell.

Braverman, H. (1974). *Labour and Monopoly Capital: The Degradation of Work in the Twentieth Century*, New York: Monthly Review Press.

Brechin, A., Liddiard, P. and Swain, J. (eds) (1981). *Handicap in a Social World*. London: Hodder and Stoughton.

Brittan, S. (1977). *The Economic Consequences of Democracy*, London: Temple Smith.

Brittan, S. (1985). '. . . and the same old problems', *Encounter*, April.

Brown, C. (1984). *Black and White Britain*. London: Heinemann/PSI.

Brown, C. and Gay, P. (1985). *Racial Discrimination Seventeen Years After the Act*. London: PSI.

Brown, C. V. (1983). *Taxation and the Incentive to Work*. Oxford: Oxford University Press.

Brown, M. and Madge, N. (eds) (1982). *Despite the Welfare State*. London: Heinemann.

Brown, G. (1989). *Where There is Greed*. Edinburgh: Mainstream Publishing.

Brown, P. (1990). 'The "Third Wave": education and the ideology of parentocracy'. *British Journal of Sociology of Education*, vol. 111, no.1, 65–85.

Brown, P. and Sparks, R. (eds) (1989). *Beyond Thatcherism: Social policy, politics and society*. Milton Keynes: Open University Press.

Bruegel, I. (1988). 'Sex and Race in the Labour Market'. Unpublished paper presented at CSE sex and class group.

Buchanan, D. and McCalman, J. (1989). *High Performance Work Systems: The Digital Experience*. London: Routledge and Kegan Paul.

Buckle, J. (1971). *Work and Housing of Impaired Persons in Great Britain*. London: HMSO.

Burgess, R. (1986). *Sociology, Education and Schools*. London: Batsford.

Burghes, L. (1987). *Made in the USA: a Review of Workfare, the Compulsory Work for Benefits Regime*. London: Unemployment Unit.

Burrows, R. (ed.) (1990). *The Enterprise Culture*, London: Routledge and Kegan Paul.

Bynner, J. (1990). 'Transition to work: results from a longitudinal study of young people in four British labour markets', in Ashton, D. N. and Lowe, G. S. (eds), *Making Their Way: Education, Training and Labour Markets in Canada and Britain*. Milton Keynes: Open University Press.

Byrne, D. (1987). 'Rich and poor: the growing divide' in Walker, A. and Walker, C. (eds), *The Growing Divide: A Social Audit 1979–1987*. London: Child Poverty Action Group.

Bytheway, B. (1985). *Induced Voluntary Early Retirement*. Unit for Life Course Analysis, University College of Swansea.

Cain, L. (1987). 'Age status and generational phenomena', *Gerontologist*, June 1987.

Casey, B. (1986). 'The "dual apprenticeship" system and the recruitment and Retention of Young Workers in West Germany' *British Journal of Industrial Relations*, vol. 24, no. 1, 63–84.

Casey, B. (1987). 'The extent and nature of temporary employment in Great Britain', *Policy Studies*, vol. 8, July.

Casey, B. and Creigh, S. (1988). 'Self-employment in Great Britain: its definition in the Labour Force Survey, in tax and social security law and in labour law', *Work, Employment and Society*, vol. 2, no.3.

Castells, M. (1978). *City, Class and Power*. Basingstoke: Macmillan.

Central Statistical Office (1988). *Social Trends*. London: HMSO.

Central Statistical Office (1989). *Social Trends*. London: HMSO.

Chapman, P. and Tooze, M. (1987). *The Youth Training Scheme in the United Kingdom*. Aldershot: Avebury.

Cliff, D. R. (1989). 'Quality of life in early retirement'. Paper presented to British Sociological Association Conference, 1989.

Cobb, S. and Kasl, J. (1977). *The Consequences of Job Loss*. Washington: US Department of Health, Education and Welfare.

Cockburn, C. (1983). *Brothers*. London: Pluto.

Cockburn, C. (1987). *Two Track Training*. Basingstoke: Macmillan.

Coffield, F., Borrill, C. and Marshall, S. (1986). *Growing Up at the Margins*. Milton Keynes: Open University Press.

Cornes, P. (1988). 'The role of work in the socialisation of young people with disabilities in a post-industrial society', Paper presented at OECD Conference 'Adult Status for Youth with Disabilities', Sigtuna, Sweden.

Coyle, A. (1987). *Dirty Business*. West Midlands Low Pay Unit.

Cragg, A. and Dawson, T. (1981). *Qualitative Research Among Homeworkers*, Department of Employment Research Paper, No. 21. London: HMSO.

Cragg, A. and Dawson, T. (1984). *Unemployed Women*, Department of Employment Research Paper, No. 47. London: HMSO.

Cross, M. (1987). 'Black youth and the YTS: the policy issues' in Cross, M. and Smith, D. (eds), *Black Youth Futures: Ethnic Minorities and the Youth Training Scheme*. Leicester: National Youth Bureau.

Cross, M. (1989). 'Blacks, Asians and labour market change', Paper presented to the ESRC Seminar on 'Social Change: Theories, Concepts, Issues', University of Surrey, 3–4 April.

Cross, M. and Johnson, M. (1988). *Race and the Urban System*. Cambridge: Cambridge University Press.

Crouch, C. (1979). 'The State, capital and liberal democracy', in Crouch, C. (ed.) *State and Economy in Contemporary Capitalism*. London: Croom Helm.

Crozier, B. (1979). *The Minimum State*. London: Hutchinson.

Curran, M. M. (1988). Gender and Recruitment, *Work Employment and Society*, vol. 2, 335–351.

Dahrendorf, R. (1987). 'The Underclass and the Future of Britain – lecture delivered at St. George's Chapel, Windsor Castle, 27 April.

Dale, A. and Bamford, C. (1988). 'Temporary workers: cause for concern or complacency?', *Work, Employment and Society*, vol. 2, no.2.

Davis, K. (1986). 'DISABILITY and the BOMB – The Connection' Clay Cross Derbyshire Coalition of Disabled People Newsletter.

Deakin, B. and Pratten, C. (1987). 'Economic effects of YTS', *Employment Gazette*, vol. 95, no.1, 31–35.

Dean, H. (1990). *Social Security and Social Control*. London: Routledge and Kegan Paul.

Department of Employment (1988a). 'New entrants to the labour market in the 1990s', *Employment Gazette*, vol. 96, no.5.

Department of Employment (1988b). 'Ethnic origins and the labour market', *Employment Gazette*, March, 164–167.

Dex, S. (1985). *The Sexual Division of Work*. Brighton: Wheatsheaf.

Dex, S. and Shaw, L. (1986). *British and American Women at Work*. London: Macmillan.

Dey, I. (1989). 'Flexible "parts" and rigid "fulls": the limited revolution in work-time patterns', *Work, Employment and Society*, vol. 3, no.4.

Disability Alliance (1987). *Poverty and Disability: Breaking the Link*. London: Disability Alliance.

Doeringer, P. B. and Piore, M. J. (1971). *Internal Labor Markets and Manpower Analysis*. Lexington: D. C. Heath.

Dombois, R. (1989). 'Flexibility by law? The West German employment promotion act and temporary employment', *Cambridge Journal of Economics*, vol. 13, 359–371.

Dore, R. (1976). *The Diploma Disease*. London: George Allen and Unwin.

Durkheim, E. (1964). *The Social Division of Labour*. New York: Free Press.

Elger, T. (1987). 'Flexible futures, new technology and the contemporary transformation of work', *Work, Employment and Society*, vol. 1, no.4, 205–222.

Ellwood, D. (1989). 'The origins of "dependency": Choices, confidence or culture?' in 'Defining and Measuring the Underclass' (Special Issue). *Focus*, vol. 12, no.1. University of Wisconsin - Madison Institute for Research on Poverty.

Employment Gazette (1978). 'Age and redundancy'. *Employment Gazette*, September 1978, 1032–1039.

Erlanger, H. and Roth, W. (1985). 'Disability policy: the parts and the whole' *American Behavioral Scientist*, vol. 28, no.3.

ESRC (1987). *Newsletter*. no.61, November.

Evans, S. and Lewis, R. (forthcoming) 'Destructuring and deregulation in the construction industry' in Tailby, S. and Whitston, C. (eds), *Manufacturing Change: Industrial Relations and Industrial Restructuring*. Oxford: Basil Blackwell.

Fevre, R. (1987). 'Subcontracting in steel', *Work, Employment and Society*, vol. 1, no.4.

Fevre, R. (1989). *Wales is Closed*. Nottingham: Spokesman Books.

Fevre, R. (forthcoming). *The Sociology of Labour Markets*. London: Harvester.

Field, F. (1989). *Losing Out: The Emergence of Britain's Underclass*. Oxford: Blackwell.

Finegold, D. and Sockice (1988). 'The failure of training in Britain: analysis and prescription', *Oxford Review of Economic Policy*, vol. 4, no.3, 21–53.

Fineman, S. (1987). 'The middle class, unemployment and underemployment', in Fineman, S. (ed.) *Unemployment: Personal and Social Consequences*. London: Tavistock.

Finkelstein, V. (1980). *Attitudes and Disabled People: Issues for Discussion*. New York: World Rehabilitation Fund.

Finkelstein, V. (1981). 'Disability and the helper–helped relationship', in Brechin, A., Liddiard, P. and Swain, J. (eds) *Handicap in a Social World*. London: Hodder and Stoughton.

Forder, A., Caslin, T., Ponton, T. and Walklate, S. (1984). *Theories of Welfare*. London: Routledge and Kegan Paul.

Finn, D. (1987). *Training Without Jobs*. London, Basingstoke: Macmillan.

Ford, J. (1989). 'Casual Work and Owner Occupation', *Work, Employment and Society*, vol. 3, no.1.

Forester, T. (1987). *The High-Tech Society*. Oxford: Blackwell.

Foucault, M. (1977). *Discipline and Punish: the Birth of the Prison*. Harmondsworth: Penguin.

Fox, A. (1974). *Beyond Contract: Work, Power and Trust Relations*. London: Faber and Faber.

Freeman, R. B. (1976). *The Over-educated American*. New York: Academic Press.

Friedman, A. (1978). *Industry and Labour*. London: Macmillan.

Fry, E. (1987). 'Disabled People and the 1987 General Election'. London: Spastics Society.

Fryer, D. M. and Payne, R. L. (1986). 'Being unemployed: a review of the literature and the psychological experience of unemployment', in Coopy, C. L. and Robertson, I. (eds) *Review of Industrial and Organizational Psychology*, Chichester: Wiley.

Funk, R. (1987). 'Disability rights: from caste to class in the context of civil rights', in

Gartner, A. and Joe, T. (eds), *Images of the Disabled, Disabling Images*. New York: Praeger.

Gallie, D. (ed.) (1988). *Employment in Britain*. Oxford: Blackwell.

Gallie, D. and Vogler, C. (1988). 'Labour market deprivation, welfare and collectivism', *Social Change and Economic Life Initiative*, Working Paper.

Gamble, A. (1988). *The Free Economy and the Strong State*. Basingstoke: Macmillan.

Gartner, A. and Joe, T. (eds) (1987). *Images of the Disabled, Disabling Images*. New York: Praeger.

George, V. and Wilding, P. (1984). *The Impact of Social Policy*. London: Routledge and Kegan Paul.

Gerry, C. (1985). 'The working class and small enterprises in the UK recession', in Redclift, N. and Mingione, E. (eds), *Beyond Employment*. Oxford: Blackwell.

Gershuny, J., Miles, I., Jones, S., Mullins, C., Thomas, G. and Wyatt, S. (1986). 'Preliminary analyses of the 1983/4 ESRC time budget data', *Quarterly Journal of Social Affairs*, vol. 2, 13–39.

Gill, C. (1985). *Work, Unemployment and the New Technology*. Oxford: Polity Press.

Government Actuary Department. (1986). *Occupational Pensions Schemes, 1983*. London: HMSO.

Graebner, W. (1980). *A History of Retirement*. New Haven, Conn.: Yale University Press.

Grover, R. and Gladstone, E. (1981). *Disabled People: A Right to Work*. London: Bedford Square Press.

Habermas, J. (1971). *Toward a Rational Society*, London: Heinemann.

Hakim, C. (1979). *Occupational Segregation*, Department of Employment Research Paper, No. 9. London: HMSO.

Hakim, C. (1982). 'The social consequences of high unemployment', *Journal of Social Policy*, vol. 11, no.4, 433–467.

Hakim, C. (1987). *Home-based Work in Britain*, Department of Employment Research Paper, No. 60. London: HMSO.

Hakim, C. (1989). 'Workforce restructuring, social insurance coverage and the black economy' *Journal of Social Policy*. vol. 18, no.4.

Hakim, C. (1988). 'Self-employment in Britain: a review of recent trends and current issues', *Work, Employment and Society*, vol. 2, no.4.

Hakim, C. and Dennis, R. (1982). *Homeworking in Wages Council Industries*, Department of Employment Research Paper, No. 37, London: HMSO.

Hall, S. and Jacques, M. (eds) (1983). *The Politics of Thatcherism*, London: Lawrence and Wishart.

Hall, S. and Jacques, M. (1989). *New Times*. London: Lawrence and Wishart.

Handy, C. (1984). *The Future of Work*. Oxford: Blackwell.

Haralambos, M. (ed.) (1985). *Sociology: New Directions*. Ormskirk: Causeway Press.

Harrington, M. (1962). *The Other America: Poverty in the United States*. Harmondsworth: Penguin.

Harris, C. C. (1987). *Redundancy and Recession*. Oxford: Blackwell.

Harris, C. C. (1989). 'The state and the market', in Brown, P. and Sparks, R. (eds), *Beyond Thatcherism*. Milton Keynes: Open University Press.

Harris, C. C. and Morris, L. D. (1986). Labour markets and the position of women, in Crompton, R. and Mann, M. (eds) *Gender and Stratification*. Oxford: Polity Press and the Swansea Unemployment Group.

Hartley, J. (1987). 'Managerial unemployment: the wife's perspective and role', in Fineman, S. (ed.) *Unemployment: Personal and Social Consequences*. London: Tavistock.

Hayes, J. and Nutman, P. (1981). *Understanding the Unemployed: The Psychological Effects of Unemployment*. London: Tavistock.

Heath, A. and McDonald, S. K. (1987). 'Social change and the future of the left', *Political Quarterly*, vol. 58, no.4, 364–377.

Herget, H. (1986). *The Transition of Young People into Employment After Completion of Apprenticeship in the 'Dual System'*, Findings from a Research Project of the Federal Institute of Vocational Training. Berlin: European Centre for the Development of Vocational Training (CEDEFOP).

HMSO (1984). *Labour Force Survey, 1983*. London: HMSO.

Hoad, A. (1986). *The Impact of Transport on the Quality of Life and Lifestyles of Young People with Physical Disabilities*. London: London School of Hygiene and Tropical Medicine.

Hogarth, T. and Daniel, W. W. (1988). *Britain's New Industrial Gypsies*, PSI Research Report No. 688. London: Policy Studies Institute.

Hudson, R. and Williams, A. (1989). *Divided Britain*. London: Belhaven Press.

Humphries, J. and Rubery, J. (1988). 'Recession and exploitation', in Jenson, J., Hagen, E. and Reddy, C. (eds), *Feminization of the Labour Force*. Oxford: Polity.

Hunt, P. (1980). *Gender and Class Consciousness*. London: Macmillan.

Illich, I. (1973). *Tools for Conviviality*. London: Calder and Boyars.

Illsley, R. (1981). 'Problems of dependency groups: the care of the elderly, the handicapped and the chronically ill', *Social Science and Medicine*. vol. 15A.

Jahoda, M. (1982). *Employment and Unemployment: A Social Psychological Analysis*. London: Cambridge University Press.

Jarvis, V. and Prais, S. (1988). *Two Nations of Shopkeepers – Training for Retailing in France and Britain*. Discussion Paper 140. London: National Institute for Economic and Social Research.

Jenkins, R. (1985). 'Black workers in the labour market: the price of recession', in Roberts, B., Finnegan, R. and Gallie, D. (eds), *New Approaches to Economic Life*. Manchester: Manchester University Press.

Johnson, P. (1988). *The Labour Force Participation of Older Men in Britain*, Discussion Paper 284, December. London: Centre for Economic Policy Research.

Jolly, S. (1980). *Age as a Factor in Employment*. Department of Employment Research Paper 11. London: HMSO.

Jordan, B. (1974). *Poor Parents: Social Policy and the 'Cycle of Deprivation'*. London: Routledge and Kegan Paul.

Jordan, B. (1973). *Paupers: the Making of the Claiming Class*. London: Routledge and Kegan Paul.

Joseph, K. (1972). Speech to the Pre-School Playgroups Association, 29 June.

Joshi, H. (1984). *Women's participation in Paid Work*, Department of Employment Research Paper No. 45. London: HMSO.

Krahn, H. J. and Lowe, G. S. (1988). *Work, Industry and Canadian Society*. Scarborough, Ontario: Nelson.

Keep, E. (1986). *Designing the Stable Door – A Study of how the Youth Training*

Scheme was Planned, Warwick Papers in Industrial Relations, No. 8, Industrial Relations Research Unit, University of Warwick.

Labour Force Survey – Preliminary Results (1989). *Employment Gazette*, Department of Employment, April.

Laclau, E. and Mouffe, C. (1985). *Hegemony and Socialist Strategy. Towards a Radical Democratic Politics*. London: Verso Press.

Laczko, F. (1987). 'Older workers, unemployment and the discouraged worker effect', in Di Gregorio, S. (ed.), *Social Gerontology, New Directions*. London: Croom Helm.

Land, H. (1976). 'Social Security and the division of unpaid work within the home and paid employment in the labour market', *Social Security Research*. London: HMSO.

Land, H. (1981). 'The family wage', in Evans, M. (ed.), *The Woman Question*. London: Fontana.

Lane, C. (1988). 'Industrial change in Europe: the pursuit of flexible specialisation in Britain and Germany', *Work, Employment and Society*, vol. 2, no.2, 141–164.

Leadbeater, C. and Lloyd, J. (1987). *In Search of Work*. Harmondsworth: Penguin.

Lee, D. (1979). 'Craft Unions and the Force of Tradition', *British Journal of Industrial Relations*, vol. 17.

Lee, D. (1989). 'The transformation of training and the transformation of work in Britain', in Wood, S. (ed.), *The Transformation of Work*, London: Unwin Hyman.

Lee, D., Marsden, D., Rickman, P. and Duncombe, J. (1990). *Scheming for Youth – a Study of YTS in the Enterprise Culture*. Milton Keynes: Open University Press.

Lee, G. and Wrench, J. (1983). *Skill Seekers: Black Youth, Apprenticeships and Disadvantage*. Leicester: National Youth Bureau.

Le Grand, J. and Robinson, R. (eds) (1984). *Privatisation and the Welfare State*. London: Allen and Unwin.

Le Gros Clark, F. and Dunne, A. C. (1955). *Ageing in Industry*. Oxford: Nuffield Foundation.

Leighton, P. (1987). 'Education: managing the workers', *Manpower Policy and Practice*, vol. 3, no.1.

Lewis, J. (ed.) (1982). *Women's Welfare, Women's Rights*. London: Croom Helm.

Lewis, O. (1965). *The Children of Sanchez*. Harmondsworth: Penguin.

Lewis, O. (1968). *La Vida*. London: Panther.

Liebow, E. (1967). *Tally's Corner: a study of Negro streetcorner men*. London: Routledge and Kegan Paul.

Lindley, R. (1983). 'Active manpower policy' in Bain, G. S. (ed.), *Industrial Relations in Britain*. Oxford: Basil Blackwell.

Lonsdale, S. (1986). *Work and Inequality*. London: Longman.

Lonsdale, S. and Walker, A. (1984). *A Right to Work: Disability and Employment*. London: Disability Alliance and Low Pay Unit.

Lyon, H. P. (1985). Late working life and retirement. Ph.D thesis. University of Wales (Swansea).

MacInnes, J. (1987). *Thatcherism at Work*. Milton Keynes: Open University Press.

Mack, J. and Lansley, S. (1985). *Poor Britain*. London: Allen and Unwin.

Mackay, R. (forthcoming). *The Welsh Economy*. Regional Studies Association.

Macnicol, J. (1987). 'In pursuit of the underclass', *Journal of Social Policy*, vol. 16, no.3.

Manning, N. (1989). *Lessons from the USA: The Legacy of Reagan's Social Policy*, paper given to the Annual Conference of the Social Policy Association. University of Bath, 10–12 July.

Marginson, P., Edwards, P. K., Martin, R., Purcell, J. and Sisson, K. (1988). *Beyond the Workplace: managing industrial relations in the multiestablishment enterprise.* Oxford: Basil Blackwell.

Marsden, D. (1986). *The End of Economic Man.* Brighton: Wheatsheaf.

Marsden, D. and Ryan, P. (1988). 'Where do young workers work? The distribution of employment by industry in various European economies', *British Journal of Industrial Relations*, vol. 24, no.1, 83–102.

Marsden, D. and Ryan, P. (1988a). *Youth Labour Market Structures and the Quality of Youth Employment in Major EEC Countries.* Report prepared for the Joseph Rowntree Memorial Trust, London School of Economics and Kings College, Cambridge.

Marsden, D. and Ryan, P. (1988b). 'Apprenticeship and labour market structure: UK youth employment and training in comparative context', Paper submitted to the International Symposium on Innovations in Apprenticeship and Training, OECD, Paris.

Marsh, C. (1988). 'Unemployment in Britain', in Gallie, D. (ed.) *Employment in Britain*, Oxford: Blackwell.

Martin, J. and Roberts, C. (1984). *Women and Employment*, Department of Employment and OPCS Report. London: HMSO.

Martin, J., Meltzer, H. and Elliot, D. (1988). *The Prevalence of Disability Amongst Adults.* London: HMSO.

Martin, J. and White, A. (1989). *OPCS Surveys of Disability in Great Britain – Report to: The Financial Circumstances of Disabled Adults Living in Private Households.* London: HMSO.

Martin, J., White, A. and Meltzer, H. (1989). *Disabled Adults in Private Households: Employment, Social Services and Mobility.* London: HMSO.

Marx, K. (1970). *Capital Vol. 1.* London: Lawrence and Wishart.

Marx, K. and Engels, F. (1970). *The Communist Manifesto.* New York: Pathfinder Press.

Maurice, M., Sellier, F. and Silvestre, J-J. (1986). *The Social Foundation of Economic Power - a comparison of France and Germany*, trans. Goldhammer, A. Cambridge, Massachusetts and London: MIT Press.

Mayhew, H. (1861). *London Labour and the London Poor* (4 volumes). London: Charles Griffin and Co.

McCrone, D., Elliott, B. and Bechhofer, F. (1989). 'Corporatism and the new right', in Scase, R. (ed.), *Industrial Societies: Crisis and Division in Western Capitalism and State Socialism*, London: Unwin Hyman.

McKee, L. and Bell, C. (1986). 'His unemployment her problem: the domestic consequences of male unemployment', in Allen, S. *et al.* (eds), *The Experience of Unemployment.* London: Macmillan.

McLennan, E., Pond, C. and Sullivan, J. (1983). *Low Pay, Labour's Response*, Tract 488. London: Fabian Society.

Meulders, D. and Wilkie, L. (1987). 'Labour market flexibility: critical introduction to the analysis of a concept', *Labour and Society*, vol. 12, no.1.

Michon, F. (1987). 'Time and flexibility: working time in the debate on flexibility', *Labour and Society*, vol. 12, no.1.

Middlemas, K. (1979). *Politics in Industrial Society: The Experience of the British System.* London: Andre Deutsch.

Millward, N. and Stevens, M. (1986). *British Workplace Industrial Relations 1980–1984.* Aldershot: Gower.

Mincer, J. (1962). 'Labour force participation of married women', in National Bureau of Economic Research, *Aspects of Labor Economics.* Princeton: Princeton University Press.

Mincer, J. (1966). 'Labor force participation and unemployment', in Gordon, R. A. and Gordon, M. (eds), *Prosperity and Unemployment.* New York: Wiley.

Morris, L. D. (1987). 'Constraints on gender', in *Work Employment and Society,* vol. I, 85–106.

Morris, L. D. (1988). 'Employment, the household and social networks', in Gallie, D. (ed.), *Employment in Britain,* Oxford: Blackwell.

Morris, L. D. (1989). *The Workings of the Household.* Oxford: Polity.

Morris, L. D. with Ruane, S. (1989). *Household Finance Management and the Labour Market.* Aldershot: Gower.

Morris, P. (1969). *Put Away.* London: Routledge and Kegan Paul.

Moylan, S., Miller, J. and Davies, R. (1984). 'For richer, for poorer? DSS Cohort Study of Unemployed Men', DHSS Social Research Branch Research Report No. 11. London: HMSO.

Myrdal, A. and Klein, V. (1956). *Women's Two Roles.* London: Routledge and Kegan Paul.

Murray, C. (1984). *Losing Ground: American Social Policy 1950–1980.* New York: Basic Books.

Murray, C. (1989). 'Underclass', *Sunday Times Magazine,* 26 November.

Musgrave, P. (1970). *Technical Change, the Labour Force and Education.* London: Methuen.

NEDO (1986). *Changing Work Patterns.* London: National Economic Development Office.

Noble, F. (1981). 'Redundancy statistics', *Employment Gazette,* June 1981, 260–226.

Norris, G. M. (1978). 'Unemployment, sub-employment and personal characteristics' (a) the inadequacies of traditional approaches to unemployment (b) job separation and work histories: the alternative approach', *Sociological Review,* vol. 26, 327–334.

Nowikowski, S. (1984). 'Snakes and ladders: Asian business in Britain', in Ward, R. and Jenkins, R. (eds), *Ethnic Communities in Business.* Cambridge: Cambridge University Press.

Office of Population Censuses and Surveys. (1987). *Labour Force Survey, 1987.* London: HMSO.

Office of Population Censuses and Surveys. (1987). *Labour Force Survey, 1985.* London: HMSO.

Oliver, M. (1978). 'Medicine and technology: steps in the wrong direction', *International Journal of Medical Engineering and Technology* vol. 2, no.3.

Oliver, M. (1984). 'The politics of disability', *Critical Social Policy,* 11.

Oliver, M. (1987). 'From strength to strength', *Community Care,* 19 February.

Oliver, M. (1990). *The Politics of Disablement: A Sociological Approach.* Basingstoke: Macmillan.

Oliver, M. and Zarb, G. (1989). 'The politics of disability: a new approach', *Disability, Handicap and Society,* vol. 4, no.3.

Oppenheim, C. (1988). *Poverty: The Facts*. London: Child Poverty Action Group.

Pahl, R. E. (1984). *Divisions of Labour*. Oxford: Blackwell.

Pahl, R. E. (1988). 'Some remarks on informal work, social polarization and the social structure', *International Journal of Urban and Regional Research*, vol. 12, no.2.

Pahl, R. and Wallace, C. (1985). 'Forms of work and privatisation on the Isle of Sheppey', in Roberts, B., Finnegan, R. and Gallie, D. (eds), *New Approaches to Economic Life*. Manchester: Manchester University Press.

Panitch, L. (1980). 'Recent theorisations of corporatism: reflections on a growth industry', *British Journal of Sociology*, vol. 31, no.2.

Parker, S. R. (1980). *Older Workers and Retirement*. London: HMSO.

Parker, S. R. (1982). *Work and Retirement*. London: Allen and Unwin.

Parkin, F. (1979). *Marxism and Class Theory: A Bourgeois Critique*. London: Tavistock.

Payne, J. (1987). 'Does unemployment run in families: some findings from the General Household Survey', *Sociology*, vol. 21, no.2, 199–214.

Perry, P. (1976). *The Evolution of British Manpower Policy*. London: British · Association for Commercial and Industrial Education.

Phillips, A. and Taylor, B. (1980). 'Sex and skill', *Feminist Review*, vol. 6, 79–88.

Phillipson, D. (1978). *The Emergence of Retirement*.

Pleck, J. H. (1985). *Working Wives/Working Husbands*. London: Sage.

Piore, M. J. and Sabel, C. F. (1984). *The Second Industrial Divide: Possibilities for Prosperity*. New York: Basic Books.

Pollert, A. (1987). The 'Flexible Firm': a Model in Search of Reality (or a policy in search of practice?'). Warwick Paper in Industrial Relations, No. 19. University of Warwick: Industrial Relations Research Unit.

Pollert, A. (1988a). 'The flexible firm: fixation or fact?' *Work Employment and Society*, vol. 2, 281–316.

Pollert, A. (1988b). 'Dismantling flexibility', *Capital and Class*, no.34, May.

Pollert, A. (ed.) (forthcoming). *Farewell to 'Flexibility': Questions of Restructuring Work and Employment*. Oxford: Basil Blackwell.

Pond, C. (1989). 'The changing distribution of income, wealth and poverty', in Hamnett, C., McDowell, L. and Saree, P. (eds), *The Changing Social Structure*. London: Sage.

Potter, T. (1987). *Flexible Labour, Temporary Workers and the Trade Union Response*. Birmingham: West Midlands Low Pay Unit.

Prais, S. (1981). *Productivity and Industrial Structure*. Cambridge: Cambridge University Press.

Raffe, D. (1986). 'Change and continuity in the youth labour market – a critical review of structural explanations of youth unemployment' in Allen, S., Watson, A., Purcell, K. and Wood, S. (eds), *The Experience of Unemployment*. London, Basingstoke: Macmillan.

Raffe, D. (1987). 'Youth unemployment in the United Kingdom', in Brown, P. and Ashton, D. N. (eds), *Education, Unemployment and the Labour Market*. Lewes: Falmer.

Rajin, A. and Pearson, R. (1986). *UK Occupation and Employment Trends to 1990*. London: HMSO.

Rees, G. and Rees, T. (1982). 'Juvenile Unemployment and State Intervention Between the Wars', in Rees, T. and Atkinson, P. (eds), *Youth Unemployment and State Intervention*. London: Routledge and Kegan Paul.

Reiser, S. (1978). *Medicine and the Rise of Technology*. New York: Cambridge University Press.

Rentoul, J. (1987). *The Rich Get Richer*. London: Unwin Hyman.

Reubens, B. (1973). German Apprenticeship: Controversy and Reform. *Manpower*, U.S. Department of Labor, vol. 5, no.11.

Richardson, J. (1985). 'The sociology of race', in Haralambos, M. (ed.) Sociology: New Direction. Ormskirk: Causeway Press.

Riddell, P. (1985). *The Thatcher Government*. Oxford: Blackwell.

Rimmer, L. (1980). *The Distribution of Income Within the Family*. SSRC Social Security Workshop Paper, September.

Roberts, K. (1984). *School Leavers and Their Prospects: Youth and the Labour Market in the Nineteen-Eighties*. Milton Keynes: Open University Press.

Roberts, K., Dench, S. and Richardson, D. (1988). 'Youth unemployment in the 1980s', in Coles, R. (ed.), *Youngs Careers*. Milton Keynes: Open University Press.

Roberts, K., Dench, S. and Richardson, D. (1986). *The Changing Structure of Youth Labour Markets*, Research Paper No. 59, Department of Employment, London: HMSO.

Robinson, O. (1988). 'The changing labour market', in Walby, S. (ed.), *Gender Segregation at Work*, 114–134. Milton Keynes: Open University Press.

Robinson, J. and Wallace, J. (1984). 'Growth and utilization of part-time labour in Great Britain', *Employment Gazette*, September.

Rose, J., in association with Deakin, N. and others (1969). *Colour and Citizenship*. London: Oxford University Press.

Rosenberg, S. (ed.) (1989). *The State and the Labor Market*. New York: Plenum Press.

Rowntree, B. S. (1901). *Poverty. A Study of Town Life*. London: Macmillan.

Rubery, J. (1988). 'Employers and the labour market', in Gallie, D. (ed.), *Employment in Britain*. Oxford: Blackwell.

Rubery, J. and Tarling, R. (1988). 'Women's employment in declining Britain', in Rubery, J. (ed.), *Women and Recession*. London: Routledge and Kegan Paul.

Rubery, J., Tarling, R. and Wilkinson, F. (1987). 'Flexibility, marketing and the organisation of production', *Labour and Society*, vol. 12, 131–151.

Ryan, J. and Thomas, F. (1980). *The Poliltics of Mental Handicap*. Harmondsworth: Penguin.

Ryan, M. (1988). 'A last civil rights battle', *The Guardian*, 20 July.

Ryan, P. (1981). 'Segmentation, duality and the internal labour market', in Wilkinson, F. (ed.), *Dynamics of Labour Market Segmentation*. New York: Academic Press.

Ryan, P. (1986). 'Apprentices, Employment and Industrial Disputes in Engineering in the 1920s'. Paper presented to Workshop on Child Labour and Apprenticeship, University of Essex, Colchester.

Sabel, C. (1982). *Work and Politics*. Cambridge: Cambridge University Press.

Sarre, P. (1989). 'Recomposition of the class structure', in Hamnett, C., McDowell, C. and Sarre, P. (eds), *The Changing Social Structure*. London: Sage.

Scase, R. (1989). (ed.) *Industrial Societies*. London: Unwin Hyman.

Scase, R. and Goffee, R. (1987). *The Real World of the Small Business Owner*. London: Croom Helm.

Schweikert, K. (1982). *Vocational Training of Young Migrants in the FDR*. Berlin: European Centre for the Development of Vocational Training (CEDEFOP).

Shearer, A. (1981). *Disability: Whose Handicap*. Oxford: Blackwell Scientific.

Sheldrake, J. and Vickerstaff, S. (1987). *The History of Industrial Training in Great Britain*. Aldershot: Avebury.

Smith, D. (1977). *Racial Disadvantage in Britain*. Harmondsworth: Penguin.

Smith, R. (1987). *Unemployment and Health*. Oxford: Oxford University Press.

Sokolowska, M., Ostrowska, A. and Titkow, A. (1981). 'Creation and removal of disability as a social category: the case of Poland', in Albrecht, G. (ed.) *Cross National Rehabilitation Policies: A Sociological Perspective*. London: Sage.

Stedman-Jones, G. (1971). *Outcast London*, Oxford: Clarendon Press.

Stone, K. (1983). 'Motherhood and waged work: West Indian, Asian and white mothers compared', in Phizacklea, A. (ed.), *One Way Ticket*. London: Routledge and Kegan Paul.

Streeck, W., Hilbert, J., Kevelaer, K-H, Maier, F. and Weber, H. (1987). *The Role of the Social Partners in Vocational Training and Further Training in the Federal Republic of Germany*. Berlin: European Centre for the Development of Vocational Training (CEDEFOP).

Streeck, W. (1989). 'Skills and the limits of neo-liberalism: the enterprise of the future as a place of learning', *Work, Employment and Society*, vol. 3, no.1, 89–104.

Taylor, R. (1979). *Medicine Out of Control*. Melbourne: Sun.

Therborn, G. (1986). *Why Are Some People More Unemployed Than Others*. London: Verso.

Therborn, G. (1989). 'The two-thirds, one-third society', in Hall, S. and Jacques, M. (eds), *New Times*. London: Lawrence and Wishart.

Titmuss (1963). 'The social division of welfare', in *Essays on the Welfare State*. London: Allen and Unwin.

Topliss, E. (1979). *Provision for the Disabled*, 2nd edn. Oxford: Blackwell Scientific with Martin Robertson.

Touraine, A. (1981). *The Voice and the Eye: An Analysis of Social Movements*, Cambridge: Cambridge University Press.

Townsend, P. (1982). *Inequalities in Health: the Black Report*. Harmondsworth: Penguin.

Townsend, P. (1974). 'The cycle of deprivation – the history of a confused thesis', in *The Cycle of Deprivation* (Papers presented to a National Study Conference at Manchester University, March). British Association of Social Workers, Birmingham.

Townsend, P. (1979). *Poverty in the United Kingdom*. Harmondsworth: Penguin.

Townsend, P. (1981). 'Employment and Disability', in Walker, A. and Townsend, P. (eds), op cit.

Turbin, J. (1988). State Intervention into the Labour Market for Youth: the Implementation of the Youth Training Scheme in Three Local Labour Markets, Unpublished Ph.D., University of Leicester.

Volz, J. (1983). *Vocational Training and Job Creation Schemes in France*. Berlin: European Centre for the Development of Vocational Training (CEDEFOP).

Wacquant, L. and Wilson, W. J. (1989). 'The cost of racial and class exclusion in the inner city', in Wilson, W. J. (ed.) 'The Ghetto Underclass: Social Science Perspectives (Special Issue), *Annals of the American Academy of Political and Social Science* No. 501.

Wagner, K. (1986). *The relation between Education, Employment and Productivity: a British-German Comparison*. Berlin: European Centre for the Development of Vocational Training (CEDEFOP).

Walby, S. (ed.) (1986a). *Patriarchy at Work*. Oxford: Polity.

Walby, S. (1986b). Segregation in employment in social and economic theory, in Walby, S. (ed.) op. cit.

Walby, S. (1989). 'Flexibility and the changing sexual division of labour', in Wood, S. (ed.), *The Transformation of Work*. London: Unwin Hyman.

Walker, A. (1983). 'Social policy and elderly people in Great Britain., in Guillemard, A. M. (ed.), *Old Age and the Welfare State*. London: Sage.

Walker, A. (1984). 'The political economy of privatisation', in Le Grand, J. and Robinson, R. (eds), *Privatisation and the Welfare State*. London: Allen and Unwin.

Walker, A. (1985). 'Early retirement: release or refuge from the labour market', *Quarterly Journal of Social Affairs*, vol. 1, no.3, 211–229.

Walker, A. and Townsend, P. (eds) (1981). *Disability in Britain: A Manifesto of Rights*. Oxford: Martin Robinson.

Wallace, C. (1987). *For Richer, For Poorer*. London: Routledge.

Ward, R. (1987a). 'Ethnic Entrepreneurship in Britain and Europe', in Goffee, R. and Scase, R. (eds), *Entrepreneurship in Europe*, London: Croom Helm.

Ward, R. (1987b). 'Resistance, accommodation and advantage: strategic development in ethnic business' in Lee, G. and Loveridge, R. (eds), *The Manufacture of Disadvantage*. Milton Keynes: Open University Press.

Werbner, P. (1984). 'Business on trust: Pakistani entrepreneurship in the Manchester garment trade', in Ward, R. and Jenkins, R. (eds), *Ethnic Communities in Business*, Cambridge: Cambridge University Press.

White, M. (1983). *Long-term Unemployment and Labour Markets*. London: PSI.

Wickens, P. (1987). *The Road to Nissan*. Basingstoke: Macmillan.

Wickham, A. (1986). *Woman and Training*. Milton Keynes: Open University Press.

Williams, K., Cutler, T., Williams, J. and Haslam, C. (1987). 'The end of mass production', *Economy and Society*, vol. 16, no.3.

Williamson, B. (1979). *Education, Social Structure and Development – a Comparative Analysis*. London, Basingstoke: Macmillan.

Wilson, W. J. (1987). *The Truly Disadvantaged: The Inner City, The Underclass and Public Policy*. Chicago: University of Chicago Press.

Young, M. (1952). 'Distribution of income within the family', *British Journal of Sociology*, vol. 3.

Zola, I. (1982). 'Social and cultural disincentives to independent living', *Archives of Physical Medicine and Rehabilitation*, vol. 63.

Index